Marie Neurath & Robin Kinross

The transformer: principles of making Isotype charts

Hyphen Press . London

First published by Hyphen Press, London, in 2009
'Wiener Methode and Isotype' copyright © Estate of Marie Neurath 2009
All other texts copyright © Robin Kinross 2009

The book was designed by Françoise Berserik, The Hague. The text was
typeset and made into pages by Teus de Jong, Nij Beets, in Adobe InDesign.
This text was output in the typeface Fresco Sans, designed by Fred Smeijers,
Antwerp. With some exceptions pictures were made at the Department
of Typography & Graphic Communication, University of Reading, with the
support of the Arts & Humanities Research Council and the 'Isotype revisited'
project. The book was made and printed in the Netherlands by Drukkerij
Haasbeek, Alphen aan den Rijn

ISBN 978-0-907259-40-4

www.hyphenpress.co.uk

*All rights reserved: no part of this book may be reproduced in any form, by print,
photocopy, or any other means, without written permission from the publisher*

for – as well as by – Marie Neurath

Contents

Preface, acknowledgements 6
1 Wiener Methode and Isotype: my apprenticeship
   and partnership with Otto Neurath / MN   9
2 The work of the transformer / RK & MN 77
3 Lessons of Isotype / RK 97
4 Marie Neurath (1898–1986) / RK 117
   Sources 121
   Index 123

Preface

In the years since 1971, when Isotype production was drawn to a close by Marie Neurath, there have been repeated efforts to discuss, recover, and learn from it. The main contributions to this process of commentary are surveyed at the end of this book ('Sources'). It is some tribute to the richness and suggestiveness of the work of Otto Neurath and his colleagues that it has engendered this discussion. At the same time, as an observer of the discussion over most of this period, I have the sense of a succession of repetitions, false starts, forgettings, misunderstandings. In this little book I have no intention of setting the record straight – or, to put it more exactly, laying out and sifting through all the available evidence and seeing what it could mean. This is the task of a long research project, and it is exactly such an effort of research that is presently being undertaken at the University of Reading under the title of 'Isotype revisited'. The present book attempts rather to go to the heart of Neurath's visual work and to suggest why it has enduring value. In naming the book *The transformer*, I want to point to the primary contribution of the work for anyone doing design – in the largest sense of that bedevilled word.

Neurath developed the notion of the transformer (it was 'Transformator' in German) to describe the process of analysing, selecting, ordering, and then *making visual* some information, data, ideas, implications. Now we might call this process simply 'design'; although it is 'design' in a particular sense. Rather than make any further definition, I hope that the examples and discussions presented here will explain the idea of transformation. In the wish to extrapolate from Isotype, or to include Isotype in a broad stream of design thinking, I have brought into the discussion work by others, from other areas of this field and of tangential fields. So, it is here in the process of visually configuring material – rather than in the 'rows of little men' – that the great value of Isotype lies.

This book contains an essay by Marie Neurath, who became the principal Isotype transformer. In what happened to be the last year of her life (1986), I asked Marie Neurath if she would collaborate on a book that might serve as a 'primer' of the subject. That book was never made, but she wrote the text now published here for the first time. I made the translation into English, discussed it with her, and made corrections. Also here are some comments that I asked Marie Neurath to make within a text that I wrote and published (in German) in 1982. So this book is able to present the Isotype transformer in her own voice. I hope and believe that this voice, partly in dialogue with mine, conveys the sense of thoughtfulness that is evident in the Isotype work itself. Her testimony also conveys the open-endedness of Isotype. As Marie Neurath always said, their work was continually in development, and shaped partly by the new tasks they took on.

My view is that Isotype can be continued now, not as some settled and defined system or method, but rather as an approach to design: not just in making pictorial statistics or presentations of information, but in any field of designing. In the last analysis, Isotype is a way of thinking.

Acknowledgements

This book issues from a long collaboration with the Department of Typography & Graphic Communication, University of Reading, where I was a student, postgraduate researcher, and for a year worked on the ordering of the material in the Otto and Marie Neurath Isotype Collection (I had the honour then of being the last employee of the Isotype Institute). I will always be glad that Michael Twyman, the founder and long-serving head of this Department, recognized the terrific value of Isotype and in 1971 brought its archive to Reading. He also brought Marie Neurath there for seminars with students: so without him I would not have met her. After a long break from the topic, this book has meant a return to Reading for me. For all kinds of help I am grateful to Eric Kindel, director of the 'Isotype revisited' project at the Department, with which this book has been allied. Also at Reading, Christopher Burke's enthusiasm helped to get this book moving; he then contributed substantially by making most of its pictures.

Almost all of the pictures in this book are taken from material in the archive at Reading. Apart from the work that was reproduced at the time in the books and other publications made by Neurath and his collaborators, I have reproduced some charts made for exhibition showing. With a very few exceptions, the originals for these charts – like almost all of the charts made at the Gesellschafts- und Wirtschaftsmuseum – have been lost or destroyed. These reproductions are taken from the files of small photographic prints of charts, known as the 'T files' (for 'Tafeln'), which are in the Reading archive. This is now the only record of the unpublished work of the Gesellschafts- und Wirtschaftsmuseum. In sizing these reproductions we have tried to respect the nature and the size of the original item, whether it be an exhibition chart (which came to be based on a module of 126 cm square), an adaptation of such a chart made for reproduction in a book or magazine, or books designed by the Isotype group.

ABBREVIATIONS

In the course of the book, the following publications and institutions are referred to with these abbreviations:

DBW: *Die bunte Welt* (1929)

EAS: *Empiricism and sociology* (1973)

GBS: *Gesammelte bildpädagogische Schriften* (1991)

GeWiMu: Gesellschafts- und Wirtschaftsmuseum in Wien

GUW: *Gesellschaft und Wirtschaft* (1930)

MMM: *Modern man in the making* (1939)

ÖGZ: *Österreichische Gemeinde Zeitung*

IPL: *International picture language* (1936)

SOURCES OF PICTURES

Pictures in this book are taken from the Otto and Marie Neurath Isotype Collection, Department of Typography & Graphic Communication, University of Reading, with the following exceptions: 1.07, 1.10, 1.11, 1.17, 1.46, 1.47, 2.06, 2.12, 3.10, 3.11, 3.13, 4.01 Robin Kinross; 3.07 Eric Kindel; 3.12 Baines Dixon Collection.

1

Marie Neurath

Wiener Methode and Isotype:
my apprenticeship and partnership with Otto Neurath

It is unfortunately not possible for me to give a complete and con-
nected account of my apprenticeship in pictorial statistics, which
could at the same time serve as an introduction for others.[1] Too
much has gone from my memory; although what was learned was
never forgotten and always reapplied. I am also sure that the process
of learning did not go forward step by step, rule for rule; just as the
visual work did not begin with the creation of symbols and rules, in
order to make visual statements. It was the other way round: something had to be stated visually, and the best way had to be found for
this. In retrospect it proved that, in the course of this work, one had
created a system of rules. But some moments, in which something
new occurred to me, have stayed in my memory. I will attempt to
describe them, in a chronological sequence; a sketch of my years of
learning and of collaboration may then emerge.

1. This text was written by Marie Neurath at my request, for a book about
Isotype that I was planning. The original text is a 25-page A4 typescript
headed 'Marie Neurath | Lehrling und Geselle von Otto Neurath | in Wiener
Methode und Isotype', dated June 1986. I made this translation in August
1986; MN read the translation and some corrections and changes were
made. She died in October 1986.

2. In an earlier autobiographical text, written in 1980 for Henk Mulder and not intended for publication, Marie Neurath wrote in some greater detail about this first meeting with Otto Neurath at the Siedlungsmuseum. She wrote (in my translation): 'Otto saw how impressed I was, and asked me if I could perhaps design things of this kind; but what should I say—I had never seen anything quite like it before. "But," he asked, "if I started a museum where such charts are designed, would you be willing to join in?" To which I replied, without qualifications: "yes", and I meant it. Otto went on, more to himself: "Now I know that I can do it." He started on the preparations at once.' From this it seems clear that Otto Neurath recognized instinctively and immediately that he had found just the right person to help him in the work of what they would call transformation. Marie Neurath was always extremely modest and self-effacing, but here she did suggest that Neurath would hardly have embarked on the project of the new museum without her.

The first encounter

I remember absolutely clearly the first encounter with Otto Neurath's graphic work. I was with a small group from the University at Göttingen on a visit to Vienna, shortly before the finish of my studies. My brother Kurt was living there, and had got to know Otto and Olga Neurath, and introduced me to them. One day, in early October 1924, Neurath took me round the Siedlungsmuseum [museum of estate housing]. Some of his charts were on display there. One of them showed the population density of different countries: their areas, subdivided into units, were directly comparable; the populations were shown through dots, each one of which represented a defined quantity, and which were regularly distributed over the areas; the number of points per unit of area then immediately gave the population density. The chart pleased me because the method of presentation is so illuminating, and indeed so obvious, and because it connects with the concrete situation. But the strongest impression on me was made by another chart. It showed the five largest cities of certain countries. As far as I know, no reproduction of this chart exists, nor did we ever treat this subject again. But the main features are preserved in my memory: in France, Paris dominating and the next four cities sharply descending; in Britain, London dominating, but then three almost equal industrial centres; in Germany, the much smaller Berlin dominating, followed by the large Hansa towns and the capitals of other states. Here it was not so much the manner of presentation that impressed me, but the formulation of the question: the idea of showing the five largest cities, and the anticipation of this outcome, that enabled so much of the history and character of these countries to be indicated. It was in front of this chart, that I agreed to join Neurath in the making of such visual presentations.[2] Neurath then went ahead with the founding of the Gesellschafts- und Wirtschaftsmuseum in Wien, which came into existence on 1 January 1925. I did my state exams in Göttingen in the middle of February 1925, and started my work at the Museum on 1 March 1925.

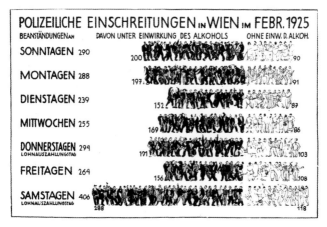

1.01 An exhibition chart, probably adapted for printed reproduction, showing interventions by police in Vienna. (ÖGZ, 15.05.1926)

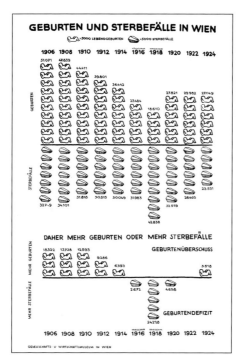

1.02 An exhibition chart, probably adapted for printed reproduction, showing births and deaths in Vienna. (T3c, ÖGZ, 15.05.1926)

Starting work

To start with I did only administration work for half days: drawing up an inventory, looking after the petty cash, typing. Meanwhile Neurath gave me the German statistical yearbook and asked me to compile various tables from it. There were two charts being made at this time, and they already showed pictorial elements. Two draughtsmen worked on them with pen and ink. Both the charts can be seen in reproduction. I cannot recall Neurath's sketches, from which the draughtsmen must have worked. In the case of the 'Polizeiliche Einschreitungen' there is no real symbol, but the rippling crowd is in fact countable; and Neurath already used an axis, in order to differentiate a markedly fluctuating group from the more stable other one. [1.01] But with the contemporaneous chart of births and deaths there is a symbol, probably for the first time. [1.02] I am sure that Neurath pro-

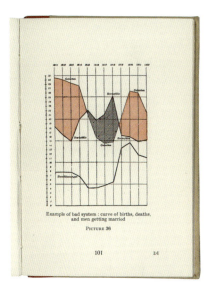

1.03 One of Otto Neurath's examples of bad method: among several difficulties here, the continuous line of the graph tells an untruth. The data here is of annual sums, but the line suggests daily or yet finer divisions; bars to represent annual data would be more honest. The word 'graph' was not allowed in Basic English, so 'curve' is used in its place. (IPL, p. 101)

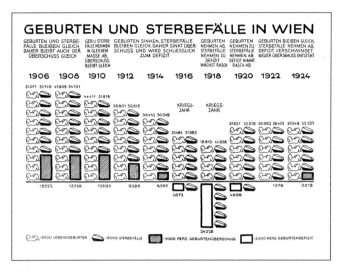

1.04

ceeded from the conventional graph form, which he reproduced in *International picture language*. [1.03] He made it clear that the statistical quantities are represented by the distance of the line from the axis, while he filled this distance with vertically arranged symbols; but then he had to separate the positions of births and deaths from each other and did that here by arranging them above and below an axis; excess or deficit of births then had to be shown in addition. There was obviously something unsatisfactory about this, and so a new version was arrived at, still with vertical arrangement of symbols, but births and deaths next to one another, so that the excess and deficit of births became clearly visible. [1.04] I remember the discussion about a further alteration to this chart. Because the two symbols used had to fill an approximately equal area, the coffin looked so small next to the baby that one could take it to be the coffin of a child. Instead of this a grave stone was then chosen as the symbol. [1.05, 1.06] Only when we had come so far as to introduce horizontal arrangement as a rule, which is usually natural and only inapplicable in exceptional cases, did this subject find its ultimate form, which was probably published first in *Die bunte Welt*. [1.07] There were now only occasional differences of opinion as to whether the excess of deaths should appear to the left or the right of the axis.

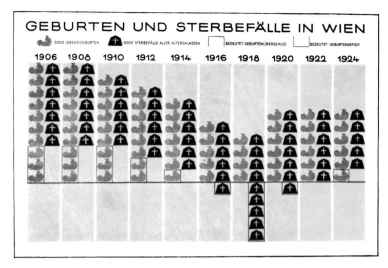

1.05

1.06

1.04–1.06 Vertically configured 'births and deaths' charts: the first two for Vienna; the third deals with Austria, and a heading points the viewer to its meaning. (1.04: ÖGZ, 15.08.1925 / 1.05: T3f, ÖGZ, 15.05.1926 / 1.06, T3d)

1.07 Births and deaths in Germany, using data shown also in 1.02: the information is now configured horizontally. (DBW, p. 43)

The first office

After the first months, in which we were tenants of the Österreichische Verband für Siedlungs- und Kleingartenwesen [Austrian association for estate-housing and small gardens], we got our own rooms in the district government office of the Third District. Here we had a large room for draughtsmen and all the processes of producing charts; the long-term collaborations of the Swiss graphic artist Erwin Bernath and the bookbinder Josef Scheer began there; and, in a smaller adjoining office, with telephone and typewriter, it now became my task to make the design drawings. I can no longer recall the preparation of our first contribution to an exhibition, about health matters (1925); my role was probably a very minor one. That was already different with the work for the 'Gesolei' (1926), a large exhibition in Düsseldorf about health care, social welfare and physical exercise ('Gesundheitswesen, Sozialfürsorge und Leibesübungen'). I remember most clearly the satisfactory way in which the age struc-

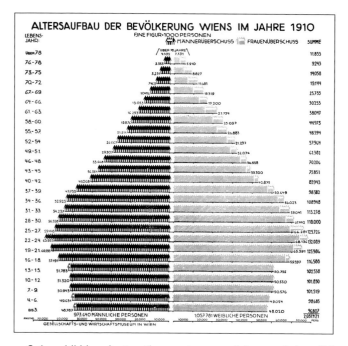

1.08 An exhibition chart on the age structure of the population of Vienna: men (dark) are on the left, women (shaded) on the right; exact numbers are still being given within the frame. (T25b, ÖGZ, 15.05.1926)

ture of the Viennese was presented, before and after the First World War. [1.08] I went with every sketch to Neurath in the next room. He had the happy ability to be entirely undisturbed by interruptions in his work; his whole attention was at once turned to my sketch, and he immediately had an idea as to how it could be improved; I then made the next attempt and put it to him again.

Most of the charts that we were commissioned to make have gone from my memory. But I still clearly remember my complete involvement with the preparation of the 'Wien und die Wiener' exhibition (1927). We had a great deal to do and for a time needed more workers. As it happened, we were offered new rooms. I travelled to and fro by bicycle between the two offices, with my sketches, the execution of which I supervised; the paying out of wages was also my job. In quieter times, between these hectic jobs, there were often special and more interesting tasks to do. For example, I worked very intensively with one of our draughtsmen (Friedrich Jahnel) on the production of the chart 'Gliederung eines industriellen Unternehmens'; most importantly, the lines connecting the different departments had to be carefully planned. [1.09] The person who had compiled the information, and who had asked us to present it graphically, was pleased that we had studied his ideas exactly, had understood and followed them, and that in turn pleased me. In these quieter periods, Neurath also had his own themes treated, such as the 'Bevölkerung der Erde' and 'Mächte der Erde'. And in 1927 there came the first black and white booklets: *Die Gewerkschaften* and *Die Entwicklung von Landwirtschaft und Gewerbe in Deutschland*.

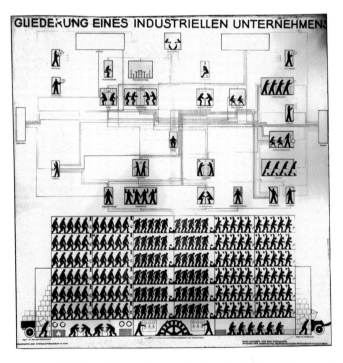

1.09 An exhibition chart on the organization of an industrial enterprise. The source is credited at the bottom right: 'Information from Emil Hitschmann, member of the Vereinigung Österreichischer Betriebsorganisatoren'. (ÖGZ, 01.05.1927)

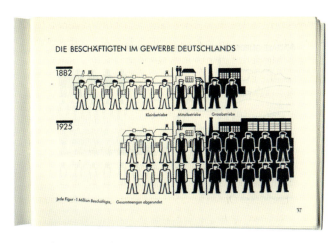

1.10 A chart on numbers of people employed in manufacturing industry in Germany, grouped by size of industrial unit, adapted for reproduction in a book. (DBW, p. 37)

Transformation

Here the themes were more interesting and made greater demands on my designing work (which only later acquired the name 'transformation'). With the chart on people employed in manufacture in Germany according to size of business, my knowledge and the constant interchange with Neurath led, within a day, to a satisfactory solution, which we never gave up. [1.10] The arrangement of symbols made it possible to see the doubling of the total number of people employed, and to be able to compare the three component groups, both in their relative portions and also in their absolute magnitudes. I remember that the last stimulus to a further improvement came from Neurath: align the middle-sized businesses under each other; then we have an axis, which makes clear the shift from small- to large-sized businesses. How much more satisfying is this solution to that in which one would show that the number of those employed in small businesses has stayed the same, that the number in middle-sized businesses has doubled and those in large concerns have multiplied by five. This is certainly worth noticing, but a stepped arrangement of symbols in rows of one, two and five would not give the impression of a com-

19

plete group and would not show that the later number is twice that of the earlier year.

This arrangement, in which one can compare the component percentage parts as well as the absolute totals, was one we always used again. Already in *Die bunte Welt* there is an example of it: the 'Bodennutzung einiger Länder'. [1.11] Here too ten units form the basis of the arrangement, from which the percentages of component parts can be easily read off; in later treatments the barren land was also made countable through squared division. There are many other examples in which the axis comes into play. One of the best charts that we ever made also belongs to this category (*Modern man in the making*). [1.12] It shows the world-empires of human history; Neurath characterized an empire as a world-empire when it ruled a quarter of mankind. In this chart, rows of twenty elements were used. There is no axis: the colour does the job that the axis would otherwise perform; it shows the geographical shift of the centres of the empire. The 'Führungsbilder' [illustrations in a chart, to suggest meanings to a viewer], using the same colours, mark out these empires, which secured their cohesion and power in different ways.

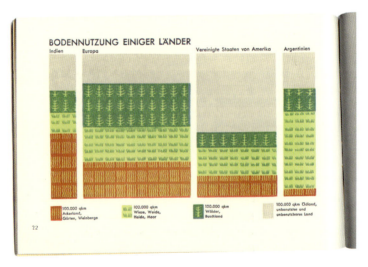

1.11 Land-use in various countries compared: another chart adapted for reproduction in a book. See 1.27 for a later treatment of this material. (DBW, p. 22)

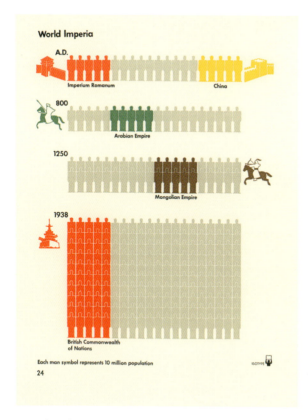

1.12 Though the theme of state power was familiar in Isotype, the topic of world-empires in history seems not to have been treated before this chart was made for the book *Modern man in the making*. (MMM, p. 24)

I was provided with good tools for my transformation work: coloured pencils and carbon-copy notebooks of roughly quarto size, in which the top sheet was squared; this was useful for my sketches, and I retained a copy of each in the book. At that time we also searched the paper shops for materials with which to make the charts. From drawing the symbols we went over to cutting them out of gummed coloured paper, which led to a simplification of forms, but which meant that each outline had to be drawn out on the back of the paper and then cut by hand. We continually worried at

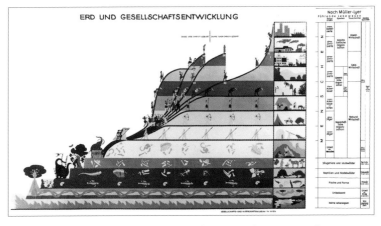

1.13 A chart showing the development of human cultures, according to the sociologist Müller-Lyer: one of the charts on display at the Volkshalle exhibition [1.14]. (T1)

the problem of how one could mechanize the production of identical symbols; perhaps with dies? This idea was quickly rejected. We thought of lino-cutting early on. But the people whom we consulted about this advised against it; they said the clarity and sharpness that Neurath wanted could not be achieved by this means. We were badly advised here. There was a hard linoleum that fully satisfied these requirements. When Gerd Arntz, an experienced wood-cutter, came to us, lino-cutting was introduced and it was maintained for our work in Vienna and the Netherlands.

The use of colour was gradually also controlled by rules. There was no technical reason for limiting the number of colours on exhibition charts. But there were other reasons. For example, Neurath came to see that the many shades of green which he had used on city-plans of Vienna often went unnoticed or were not remembered, and he decided to do without them on educational grounds. In time the rules became stronger: like the forms, colours acquired their particular educational duties, and one had to have good reasons for their application. I clearly remember the occasion on which I grasped this. We were still in our first office. While Neurath was in Germany on a lecture tour, a draughtsman (Bruno Zuckermann) and I worked together on a chart (about the phases of culture, according to Müller-Lyer), the completion of which was to greet him on his return home. [1.13] He was however very annoyed: why this many colours? What are they supposed to mean? How can you justify them? So we learned our lesson. Though Neurath still gave room to the chart and it had a special place in our main exhibition, which it kept to the end. But a certain arbitrariness in the choice of colour still persisted for a time. We had already moved into our new and final office (Ullmanstraße 44, XIV) and yet still had a 'pink group' and an 'ochre group', after their preferred colours.

The Volkshalle and the final address

Around the time of this move the Gemeinde Wien offered us the Volkshalle in the new town hall for our main exhibition. [1.14–1.15] After months of preparatory work it was opened on 7 December 1927. The installation was a welcome exercise for Neurath's design abilities. A modern museum had to be made in this gloomy neo-Gothic hall: one that attracted and satisfied visitors. Josef Frank, the consultant architect, proposed that frames and stands no longer be stained black, but left in their natural wood colour, that red carpets be laid and that lighting should not be used for the whole space but that the charts only be strongly lit. Thus just the lower space was light and the vaults disappeared in darkness, which really stayed unnoticed. For the square entrance area, which the visitor coming from the Rathausplatz first encountered, Neurath had devised a huge map of Austria as an eye-catcher. He used a novel device – magnetic symbols. He got this idea from notices, for street windows and elsewhere, whose text could be easily altered: the surface was iron and the letters magnetic. A collaboration developed with the manufacturing firm. We acquired an 8 x 4 metre sheet of iron, mounted on wood, and the magnetic pieces to place on it were squares of about 2 centimetres length, which we coloured according to the main industry groups; painted symbols showed sub-groups. But the boldest

1.14

1.15

1.14–1.15 The permanent exhibition of the Gesellschafts- und Wirtschaftsmuseum in the new town hall in Vienna: above, by day, and below, by night. It was open on Sunday (9 am to 1 pm), Thursday and Friday (5 to 7 pm).

thing about this map was that the mountainous regions of Austria were shown by a flat relief, which was cut along the 1000 metre altitude line and was placed over the appropriate areas of the map. The whole map – the still visible parts of the iron plate and the parts covered by the wood sheet – was coloured according to land use. All the magnetic symbols were on the land below 1000 metres; the wood sheet needed no iron surface. Neurath had discussed this plan for a map previously with the geographer Professor Lehmann, who had considerable objections to the strong simplification. But Neurath did not allow himself to be frightened off by this warning, and in the end Professor Lehmann was completely won over by the map and declared this in an article.

We used magnetic charts again on other occasions. Once we made a weather map of Austria for an exhibition and adapted the symbols every day to the weather report. They were also used in school teaching: for example, a map could be held by magnets on an iron sheet and magnetic symbols could be placed on it.

In the main room of the Volkshalle, to the left on the outer wall of the first bay, was our chart on the phases of culture, and the red carpet between the bays led one's attention to another extra large chart, which was concerned with housing. In the central area there was also a series of models: simplified models of housing, constructed from cut layers of wood; transparent ground plans of the storeys of a large indoor swimming pool, mounted above each other, with all the side-rooms; parks and paddling-pool areas with tree symbols turned on a lathe. These were much loved by young visitors and they were always disappearing. Neurath, however, did not want more security personnel, but rather larger supplies of these small turned trees.

I often had to take school classes round the Museum and liked to do this. I was able to ask questions, and the children could find the answers from the charts. The bays were just big enough for these groups; the charts in them could easily be compared with one another and connections made, thus enriching the information. Through these conversations one could also notice when a chart was not easy enough to understand and this taught us, the producers, something. Occasionally I also watched children who came into the Museum on their own accord. I remember a schoolboy who looked quietly at a chart; the younger sister holding his hand was not yet bored and looked at the symbols, counting them. That was an instance of the charts meaning something for everyone, that they excluded nobody, that they allowed several levels of understanding. Neurath often stressed this. Something else that Neurath valued in the museum as a means of education was that it is neutral, provides objective facts and leaves judgement and evaluation to the viewer.

At the end of the main hall there was a further, square room, that was set aside for lectures and the projection of slides and films. We made more and more slides; but hardly anything was done with films. Neurath believed that one day they would have their turn.

Die bunte Welt and *Gesellschaft und Wirtschaft*

First, however, there were more jobs to do. After the opening of the Volkshalle, a Viennese publisher appeared, wanting to take the risk of publishing a coloured book: *Die bunte Welt*. [1.16] We were busy with its preparation in 1928. The book is remarkable for its mixture of different styles and shows how rapidly we were changing at this time. We had hardly finished this little book when a new and much larger task came to us: a Leipzig publisher, the Bibliographisches Institut, wanted to bring out something special to celebrate an anniversary and turned to Neurath for ideas. Thus arose the idea of the portfolio of charts *Gesellschaft und Wirtschaft*, on which we worked for a whole year, 1929.

All sorts of things went into *Die bunte Welt*: some we had already shown before either as exhibition chart or in reproduction, and various multi-coloured things were added; too coloured, if one considers the costs of reproduction. I remember our former colleagues in the technical department; Arntz joined it just at the end of the job, working on some black and white charts and also the cover. I remember

1.16 Cover of *Die bunte Welt: Mengenbilder für die Jugend* (Vienna: Artur Wolf, 1929). The full title might be translated as 'the colourful world: pictorial statistics for young people'. The GeWiMu is given authorship credit on the book's title page. (144 x 212 mm)

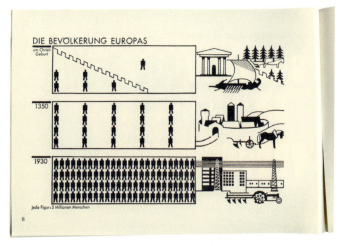

1.17 The population of Europe; the 'Führungsbilder' here are given greater prominence than would be normal later in Isotype work. (DBW, p. 8)

only a little of my own work. For example, I attempted to simplify the equal area world map. My favourite chart, 'Die Bevölkerung Europas', was essentially Neurath's idea and it shows how he taught history; my task here was just to draw a meaningful arrangement of the figures. [1.17] Some of the charts I probably did not even sketch, for when we moved to the larger office in the Fourteenth District a second person came to work on transformation with us: Friedrich Bauermeister.

The preparation of *Gesellschaft und Wirtschaft* was quite different. We had to make something that could stand up on the international market, and the publisher paid good advances. Neurath was able to hire the best specialist advisers and collaborators. As well as the statistician Dr Alois Fischer, introduced to us by Professor Lehmann, there was the historian Dr Robert Bleichsteiner from the Völkerkundemuseum, the art-historian Dr Schwieger, an assistant of Professor Strygowski, the cartographer Professor Karl Peucker, and occasionally a historian of technology, whose name I can no longer recall. They got together with us regularly, as our 'academy'; I was always there, because the transformation for this work was entrusted to me. I gained by being able to put my transformations to these specialists as well as to Neurath. Neurath had ideas of his own as to what this work should treat; the specialists delivered the material, as far as was possible, and gave advice concerning the treatment of a subject. I remember, for example, how Neurath said that the Mongols must certainly be included among the empires of world history; but what could we show, for neither cities nor production – as in the Roman Empire – had any significance for them. Dr Bleichsteiner suggested showing roads, which enabled rapid contact between the home country and the distant boundaries of the empire. This 'academy' was an experience for me: I was among people who had mastered their subjects. Once Bleichsteiner and Fischer were discussing a region in Central Asia as if they had spent their last summer holiday there. For my own part, I learned especially from Professor Peucker,

1.18 The population of the Arabian Empire and neighbouring areas (GUW, chart 7): one of a pair of charts in *Gesellschaft und Wirtschaft* on the history of this region. Ethnic groupings are denoted by colour; note the different treatments of fractions of the unit. (Dimensions of the GUW charts: 300 × 450 mm)

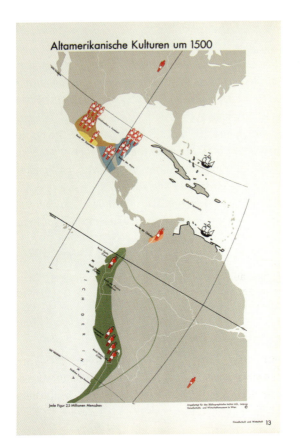

1.19 Ancient cultures of Latin America, around 1500 (GUW, chart 13). The territories of the native groupings and of Spanish imperial influence are shown with no greater visual precision than historical knowledge allowed.

the cartographer. When I showed him my simplifications of maps in *Die bunte Welt*, the equal area projection certainly seemed right to him; 'but', he said, 'we have to give the thing a bit more life'. What he meant with that I soon saw in his sketches: I had often simplified mechanically, but he indicated, on the coastline, where there were important mountainous protrusions or river outlets or delta patterns. Neurath had many new projections drawn, always equal area, which were appropriate for our quantitative presentations. He ordered world maps with different meridians in the centre, in order to see the

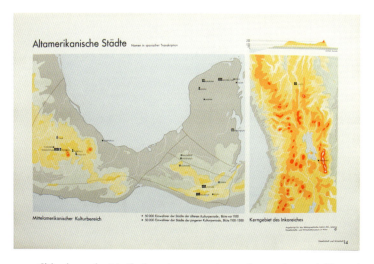

1.20 Cities in ancient Latin America, around 1500 (GUW, chart 14). The colour coding for height above sea level is explained in the elevation of the section of Inca land, on the right.

world in different perspectives. For the Arabian Empire he wanted a map in which Arabia stood in the middle like a pillar and the conquered areas spread out to the sides like wings. [1.18] With the maps of ancient cultures of Latin America we used Peucker's original suggestion of colours for the higher ground levels; they had once been adopted at an international meeting, but were then implemented incorrectly. [1.19–1.20] The idea of making a map of former and still existing forests came from Schwieger; so too the monastery map. [1.21–1.22]

In doing the separate transformations I thought of the work as a whole, more so than with previous jobs; charts that dealt with similar themes could be related to each other. We had to make a whole series of economic maps, on which production and use would be shown; the exported part of what was produced was given the symbol of a ship as a basis, and imports were shown only in outline in the country of use, so that the route of an export remained undefined. [1.23–1.24] Elsewhere the development of production, by country, was shown for a number of products. How should one give a structure to this presentation? I decided to try it with an axis, which

1.21 Forests in Europe and near-Asia (GUW, chart 34): colours are deployed to indicate known areas of forestation (dark green), 'provable areas' (yellow), areas that had 'probably once been' forests (yellow), areas of 'light forestation' (light green). Viewers are left to discuss and investigate on this basis.

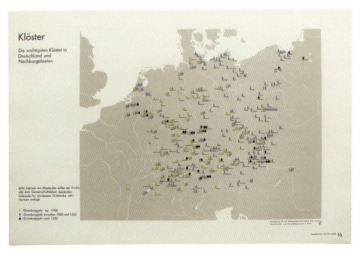

1.22 Monasteries in Europe (GUW, chart 16). Three categories of monastery are chosen, by date of founding. The expansion of numbers in the middle period (1000–1550)–the blue symbols–especially to the East, is notable.

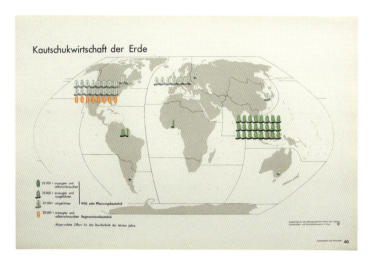

1.23 The world's rubber economy (GUW, chart 46). Outline symbols denote imports, fully coloured denote exports; orange denotes recycled rubber.

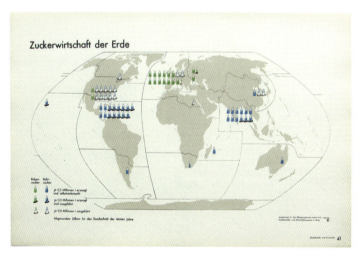

1.24 The world's sugar economy (GUW, chart 41). Sugar beet is green, raw sugar is blue; imports and exports are shown in the usual way.

33

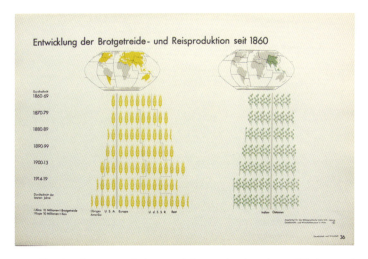

1.25 The development of wheat and rice production since 1860 (GUW, chart 36). In both parts of this chart, the choice of how to divide the material either side of the axes follows what this material itself suggests, rather than any more general rule.

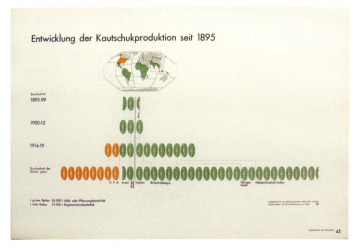

1.26 The development of rubber production since 1895 (GUW, chart 45). In its consistent symbols and colours, this forms a partner also to chart 46 [1.23].

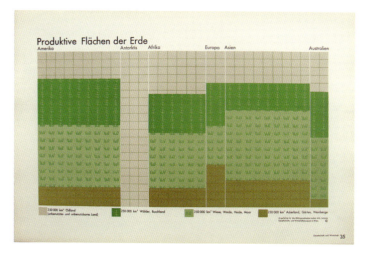

1.27 The earth's productive land (GUW, chart 35). The amount of cultivated land in different countries is here configured geographically, from west to east: contrast the earlier arrangement in 1.11. Colours are consistent with those used in chart 34 [1.21].

I placed in the Atlantic: America to the left, the rest of the world to the right, in geographical sequence from west to east – from left to right – and, within this main sequence, from north to south. A small world map over the axis indicated the basically geographic character of the arrangement. [1.25 – 1.26] We did not yet have this rule when we produced *Die bunte Welt*, as one sees, for example, on the chart of land use; here the arrangement followed the size of the share of cultivated land. [1.11, 1.27] But we soon realized that, for some comparison between countries, arrangement according to magnitude is a bad principle: one always has sequences of diminishing quantities, and the real statement has to be read from the accompanying names – not a very visual method. There are however cases in which one must arrange according to magnitude; for example, if one wants to show that infant mortality rises as income falls. [1.28] We always kept the geographical ordering principle and developed a sequence of all the countries of the world; it forms the basis also of the division of the world into eight (later six) economic areas, which was first applied in *Gesellschaft und Wirtschaft* and then always afterwards, and finally in *Modern man in the making*.

35

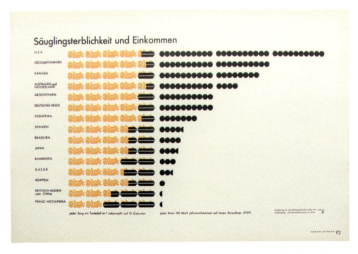

1.28 Infant mortality and income (GUW, chart 92). The point here is to show how illness and death relate to economic income, and geographical ordering takes second place. Income symbols are grouped in tens, for easy apprehension.

It became clear, to my surprise, that the hard-won arrangement for births and deaths could be applied to other subjects when I had to do the transformation for the chart about the emigration and immigration of people in important countries. [1.29] Here too excess and deficit are important: the arrangement could simply be retained, with just the symbols being altered.

Even the presentation of density found a new use: with the distribution of wealth in Germany, the population was distributed against a background of coins. [1.30] That it concerned the total wealth was indicated by arranging the coins in a closed rectangle; the captioning made clear that it dealt with the total population.

If one wants to show how a total quantity divides into component groups, the presentation must stress that it is concerned with a totality, by using the most self-contained form possible. Sometimes the statistical data one has makes that easy, as, for example, with the size of businesses in German agriculture. [1.31] Here the total of twenty-five units could be arranged in a square, in five rows each with five units, and then one of the sub-groups – the largest concerns

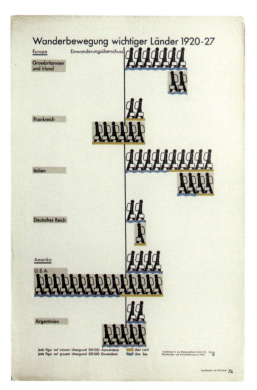

1.29 The movement of people from and to notable countries, 1920–7 (GUW, chart 74). The 'surplus and deficit' axial arrangement works perfectly for this topic; grouping the symbols (in fours, given the unit employed) would not be appropriate here.

– just filled a row. Two other sub-groups produced two-unit portions left over from full five-unit rows, and the one unit of small-holdings then helped to make up the row. The best arrangement was produced finally by giving the small-holdings the central position of the square; in that way one produced a welcome equality of balance, and made more noticeable the fact that the small and middle-sized farmers occupied as much land as the two largest categories combined. We were not always so lucky. With the charts in *Gesellschaft und Wirtschaft* that showed the social groupings of the total population, the total population could only be given an approximately closed form. [1.32]

37

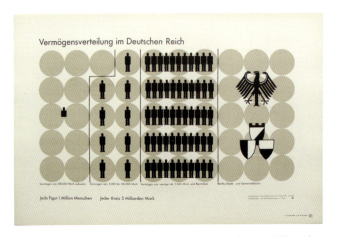

1.30 Distribution of wealth in Germany (GUW, chart 91). Three income groups are distinguished: the wealthiest to the poorest, moving from left to right. The picture is completed by state and commonly shared wealth (right).

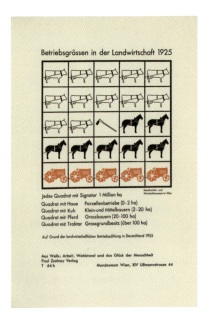

1.31 Size of agricultural concerns in Germany 1925 (T65g). The chart was published in H.G. Wells, *Arbeit, Wohlstand und das Glück der Menschheit*, 1932, and is reproduced here from a loose offprint circulated by the GeWiMu (226 x 151 mm). A second colour (red) was available, though not strictly required; it is used to emphasize 'powered cultivation'.

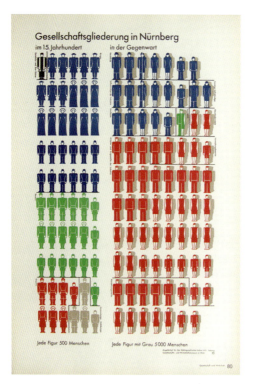

1.32 Social groupings in Nuremberg, in the fifteenth century and in the present (GUW, chart 80). Colours indicate the broad groupings: blue, the upper strata; green, those working on the land; red, the lower classes; black, those in the church; grey, others. The thousand-times greater unit value in the present-day figures is indicated by shadowed symbols. A partner (chart 81) showed social groupings in Vienna, around 1700 and in the present.

The charts on the peoples, the economic forms, and the religions of the world, also belong to this category of arrangement. [1.33–1.35] When we first made them, the world population was 1800 million, of which 600 million were white and 600 million were Mongols, with the rest combining to make 600 million also. So the division into three equal groups came quite naturally. With time, the population increased, but we stuck to the three-part division, which was still serviceable.

39

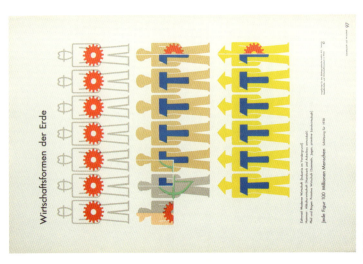

1.34

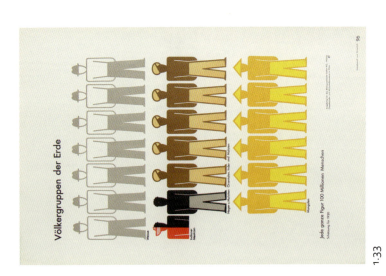

1.33

40

1.35

1.33–1.35 Population groups of the world (GUW, chart 96); Economic forms of the world (GUW, chart 97), Religions of the world (GUW, chart 98). As well as showing broad racial grouping, colour is used consistently, as always in Isotype, to support the meanings of the symbols for economic forms: red for industry, blue for older forms of work, green for 'primitive' activities.

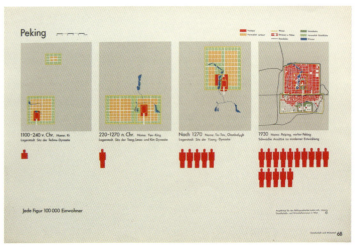

1.36

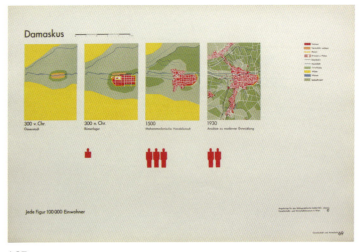

1.37

42

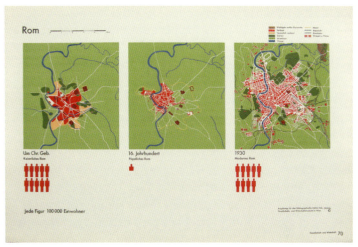

1.38

1.39

1.36–1.39 Peking (GUW, chart 68); Damascus (GUW, chart 69), Rome (GUW, chart 70), New York (GUW, chart 71). Standardization of scale and colour lets comparisons be made both within and between the four presentations.

I was especially fond of one group of four charts, showing the different characters of the development of four cities; Damascus and Rome fascinated me in particular. [1.36–1.39] Here my transformation sketches could only do part of the job. I remember how I sat beside Hans Thomas as he worked on the map of Rome and, street for street, said to him: keep, or leave out. The surviving pattern of the ancient streets had to be clearly visible in medieval and modern Rome.

In order to complete the production of the charts in the time agreed with the publisher, we were joined, most notably, by Peter Alma from Amsterdam and August Tschinkel from Prague, both of whom worked in styles similar to ours. There are thus occasional variations in the symbols, without any good reason. The time when Neurath sat down with Arntz and started a systematic review of the symbols, their interrelation and combination, came only when this large job was over and there was more leisure. So then there came into existence the basic lexicon of symbols, which were meaningful and well-formed: the result of a very fruitful collaboration, in which I myself hardly took part. But I remember, for example, the effort that went into seeing that the coffee symbol occupied a certain area, that of the rice and grain symbols too, and also that it could be halved, if necessary.

The last years in Vienna

The number of collaborators shrank again after the completion of *Gesellschaft und Wirtschaft*, and we gave up one floor of our two-storey office. There were fewer exhibitions, but we were becoming known abroad and this lead to new developments. We had to install a museum in Berlin-Kreuzberg; in Moscow, we had to give instruction in our method; and Neurath was invited to give a lecture on production capacity, with slides and exhibition charts, at the World Social Economic Congress in Amsterdam, 1931. I was only once in Berlin-Kreuzberg, when the autumn 1932 election results were announced, in order to amend a presentation made on a map of Germany. In Moscow, as well as urgent work, I had to teach transformation to a Russian woman. There was also in Vienna at that time a promising student of transformation, Heinz Kaufler, who once came to Moscow too, and who helped us out for a time in the Netherlands. The most stimulating work for our development was that for the Amsterdam Congress. The division of the world into six main economic areas was established then, and it proved itself well, for example, in the chart on the interconnections of international finance. Neurath used the 'tableau économique' of Quesnay as an example of how one could separate money and credit from production and consumption: from Quesnay's very complicated description in words, we worked out a beautifully clear schema that, like a game, made everything easy to grasp. [1.40] The new contacts with the West were essential for our future, which looked increasingly threatened, and especially with the two women who organized the Congress: Mary L. Fleddérus, from The Hague, and Mary van Kleeck, from New York. We set up branches in the Netherlands, England, and the USA.

In Vienna itself, our work with schools intensified after *Gesellschaft und Wirtschaft* became available. We had a school at our disposal for experiments and a good collaboration followed. I was once in another school and took part in the class work. We had conferences of teachers in our office and discussed what kinds of tests one could make. Examples of some of the results were included as illustrations to the book *Bildstatistik nach Wiener Methode in der Schule*, which

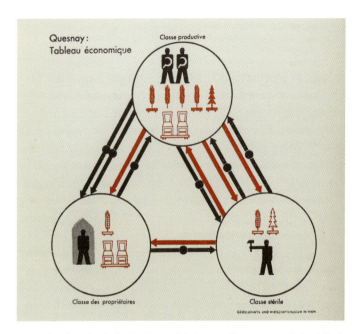

1.40 The chart included in Neurath's lecture 'Das gegenwärtige Wachstum der Produktionskapizität der Welt', in: *World social economic planning* (The Hague: International Industrial Relations Institute, 1931). Quesnay distinguished three classes in a nation: the 'productive class', which cultivates the land and pays rent to the 'proprietors', and the 'barren class', engaged in activities other than agriculture and which shows deficits. The red lines show the flow of goods between classes, the black lines show money transfer.

Neurath wrote then. At this time we heard of Basic English and came into contact with C.K. Ogden. Work started already in Vienna on the two books in Basic English, which were to be called *Basic by Isotype* and *International picture language: the first rules of Isotype*. After the publication of *Gesellschaft und Wirtschaft* an article on 'Wiener Methode' appeared in the same publisher's *Meyers Konversationslexikon*. This name was lost when we left Vienna in 1934. We could survive only as citizens of the world. Never again did we have a home like Vienna.

The Hague

The two Basic books forced us to find a new name for the method, and the formation of the word 'Basic' ('British American Scientific International Commercial') helped in this. One afternoon I sat down and played around with it. I arrived at 'International System Of Teaching in Pictures' – Isotip; that did not sound quite right yet, except for the first syllable. It was then only a short step to 'Isotype'; but I did not succeed in finding a good sequence of words for it, and we stayed with the not entirely satisfactory solution of 'International System Of TYpographic Picture Education'. When Neurath returned in the evening from a meeting in Amsterdam he was pleased with the name and, the next day, asked Arntz to design a symbol for it. Both name and symbol were then published, for the first time, in *International picture language*. [1.41]

Basic by Isotype is a primer for Basic English. [1.42] To introduce vocabulary with the help of pictures is often quite simple, for example, in the case of 'comb' and 'brush' or 'dog' and 'cat'; but with 'bread' and 'cake' we showed several of the common types of these things.

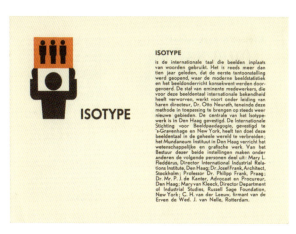

1.41 This leaflet (147 x 207 mm; the first of its four pages is shown here), which must date from around 1935, would have been the very first announcement of the name Isotype, its symbol, and its new producing organization: the International Foundation for Visual Education.

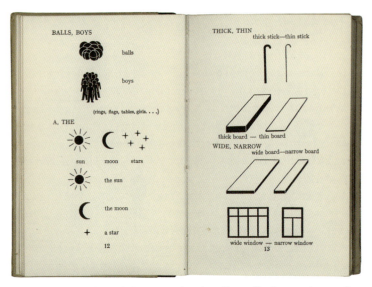

1.42 Otto Neurath, *Basic by Isotype*, London: Kegan Paul, 1937. (150 x 98 mm)

Instead of 'tree' we showed 'trees', in three different forms: a deciduous tree, conifer, and palm. One cannot make a picture of the collective concept of 'tree'. In order to explain 'a' and 'the', we first drew sun, moon, and stars; then: the sun, the moon, a star. For qualities, we gave two examples: the common quality is then the word that we mean. For example: 'young tree', 'old tree' – that could have meant 'small tree', 'large tree', or 'thin tree', 'thick tree'; so we added 'young man', 'old man'. With words such as 'between' and 'through', we showed concrete situations: 'boy between two girls'; 'boy goes through the door'. We showed family relations on a tree structure: 'parents with their children'. In short, there was a surprisingly large number of problems to solve, and the symbol-making approach of Isotype was often a great help.

When Neurath agreed to the production of a Basic primer, he asked if he could at the same time make a book about our method for this series, and Ogden agreed at once. [1.43] So we had to work on two books simultaneously; both interesting, in their different ways. After ten years' experience it was time to give a summary of our rules, and it was more extensive and more systematic than all

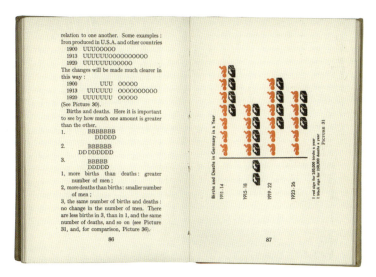

1.43 Otto Neurath, *International picture language*, London: Kegan Paul, 1936. (150 x 104 mm)

the previous ones. I was concerned with the words as well as the pictures, and, unpractised as I was, attempted to formulate it in Basic English. Miss Lockhart, the closest collaborator of C.K. Ogden, came for a few days to The Hague and lent her elegant Basic style to the whole text. We learned how difficult it is to write Basic English, and how easy to read it is; but this was just the same as with our picture language. In another way too we felt we were members of the same family, in a struggle for international communication: whether one wishes to help someone travelling in a foreign country find their way, or to establish a basis for shared knowledge. Here Neurath explained the character of our picture-language in relation to verbal language. He described Isotype as a helping language: some words of explanation are necessary in any chart. To create a language of signs, as with Chinese script, was something we never tried to do.

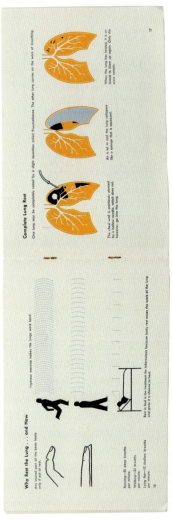
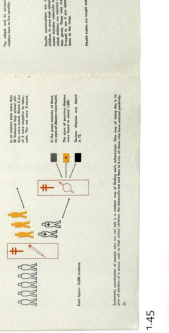

1.44–1.45 Two spreads from *Tuberculosis: basic facts in picture language* (New York: National Tuberculosis Association, 1939). This booklet accompanied the NTA's travelling poster exhibition. (153 x 230 mm)

Contact with America

We endured considerable poverty during the first years in the Netherlands. We had friends; we had exhibitions at two places in Amsterdam; Mr Kerdijk, director of Trio, a printing company in The Hague, offered us space for an exhibition and printed our booklet about world travel: nothing helped to get us commissions. The first sign of relief was the visit of an American medical man, Dr Kleinschmidt, who was responsible for educational work with the National Tuberculosis Association in New York. He had made the journey to Europe to find new ideas, in visual presentation above all, and said that he had made two discoveries, the Deutsches Hygienemuseum in Dresden and Isotype. It was not long before Neurath was invited to New York; and some weeks later he arranged for me to follow; I arrived just as Roosevelt was re-elected, in November 1936.

The Tuberculosis Association had as their office a single large room in the Rockefeller Center; desks everywhere, with enough distance between them; it was always easy to ask a specialist to come over. We quickly began to collaborate. [1.44–1.45] We soon agreed about the use of colours for meaning: orange for healthy, black for ill and causing illness, red for medical measures, light blue for the air of the pneumothorax. We discussed the simplification of the representation of the lung, and the need to give it an enclosure – without this a pneumothorax would not be conceivable. Following previous accident protection pictures, we were confident about charts such as those on possibilities of infection and on protection, but the more general requirement that an infectious invalid must be isolated demanded a more abstract presentation – one removed from the specific individual case. We surrounded the sick person with a continuous red line, indicating medical measures; this encapsuling blocked the dangerous black rays emitted from the invalid. We introduced a similar abstract presentation for the concept of 'strength of resistance'. An allegorical presentation had been used earlier. This was however not really illuminating: it showed what happens if a strong man and a weak man have to carry an easy load, and if the strong man and the weak man have to carry a heavy load. Our presentation,

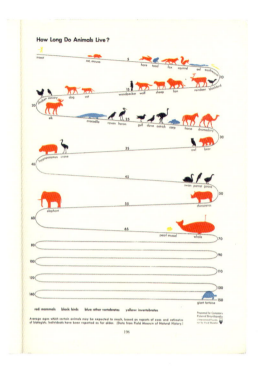

1.46 Colours are assigned to the broad categories of animal, introducing another dimension of meaning to the presentation. *Compton's pictured encyclopedia* (Chicago: F.E. Compton & Co., 1939). (255 x 191 mm)

more abstract and yet nearer to the situation, showed a strong and a weak enclosure, and what happens if a weak attack of black arrows comes from outside (repulsion in the first case, partial penetration in the second) and what happens with a strong attack (partial penetration, complete splitting up). The enclosure here is nothing more than a curved line, orange in colour, thick or thin, indicating an inside and an outside. For me this chart had something very convincing about it, and its validity is much more general than most of the other charts of the series. The 5,000 reproductions of our charts, in the size of the originals, went to all corners of the United States as a travelling exhibition, and it was reported that they were studied with great interest and understood by Inuit, Indians and everyone else alike.

When we were finished with the design of the exhibition and had

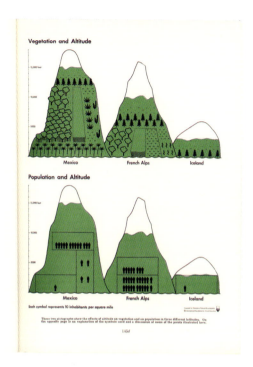

1.47 Population density and geographical description are combined in this unusual presentation. (*Compton's pictured encyclopedia*)

just to discuss a booklet presenting the same material, there came an unexpected invitation to Mexico City, where a museum for science and industry was to be started. We were there for six weeks, giving instruction: Neurath in German with a Spanish translator, and I in English to those who knew English. I found the people there very intelligent, except that they tired easily – which would have had to do with the height above sea-level of 2,400 metres. Professor Mendizabal from the Ministry of Education, who was responsible for the project of this museum, came along with all of us on a trip to a silver mine; he was an archaeologist and, on the way, took us around Teotihuacan. We were told that the mine workers survived for three years – then their lungs were destroyed by fine dust from the hard rock. I have now forgotten what else we learned; but at the time I

53

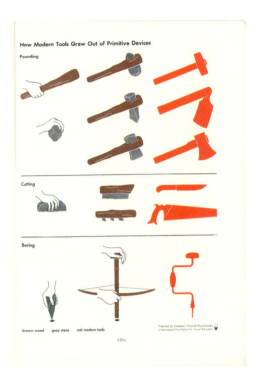

1.48 The material is organized in tabular form; red is applied to the culture of modern, mechanized times. (*Compton's pictured encyclopedia*)

made a series of drawings, which were projected on the screen to accompany Neurath's lecture in the large theatre. On the three-day train journey back to New York I did the sketches for the tuberculosis booklet, which we were then able to discuss and to conclude before our return home.

Another collaboration started soon afterwards, similarly generous in scale and based on mutual trust, with the Chicago publishers Compton, who were solely concerned with the publication of a children's encyclopedia: *Compton's Pictured Encyclopedia*. [1.46–1.48] When Neurath was there for the first meeting, they showed him the examples of illustrated works that had been gathered from around the world, and among them was *Gesellschaft und Wirtschaft*. In the few years before the War we contributed a large number of charts.

Many were of the usual kind, but some treated new subjects: for example, the effect of height above sea-level on vegetation and population in different climate zones. Here we were able to use as a partial source the beautiful Berghaus *Atlas*, which accompanied Alexander von Humboldt's *Kosmos*. Other examples concerned the natural sciences: the average age reached by animals; the circulation of carbon and nitrogen between plants and animals living together. Now we had to make clear statements about oxygen, carbon and nitrogen, as before about people and cars. A new use of symbols had to be introduced to represent the processes, and nothing was allowed to go missing from the circulation. Our discipline of picture-language was now tested in new fields. We became more confident in the belief that every kind of scientific statement is open to a visual treatment. This was the beginning. In the further course of our work we really did have to tackle physics and chemistry, geology and biology, astronomy and atomic structure. This step beyond the limits of our previous work certainly strengthened Neurath in his plan for a visual thesaurus as part of the International Encyclopedia of Unified Science.

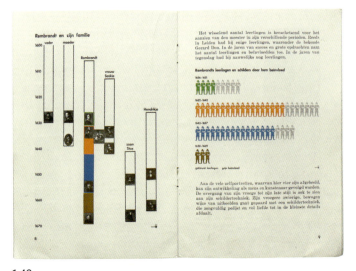

1.49

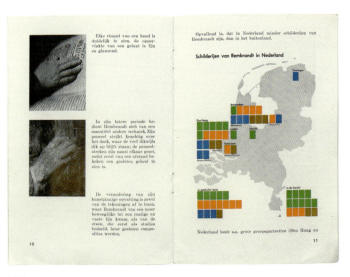

1.50

1.49–1.50 Charts made for the exhibition 'Rondom Rembrandt' were shown at the three 'Bijenkorf' department stores in 1938. The colours indicating the main phases of Rembrandt's life and work are another instance of letting meanings become evident visually, through a simple system of coding.

Last years in The Hague

Commissions now began to come from within the Netherlands too: from the Ministry of Health, for example, but also from private organizations. A large department store, De Bijenkorf, came to us for an exhibition in three copies for its three branches in Amsterdam, The Hague, and Rotterdam, and they left the choice of subject up to us. The idea was to attract a new public. I suggested the theme of 'Rembrandt' to Neurath, and he agreed at once. Frequent visits to the Mauritshuis, and above all to a room there with three Rembrandt pictures and Vermeer's 'View of Delft', had become almost a necessity of life to me. There had also recently been a special Rembrandt exhibition in Amsterdam, at which it had struck me how many opportunities to help the public had been missed, by conventional hanging, and by separating the paintings from the prints. Now, we could not show originals, but rather we had much of the environment in which this work had been made, and so our exhibition had the title 'Rondom Rembrandt' [around Rembrandt]. [1.49–1.51] We showed

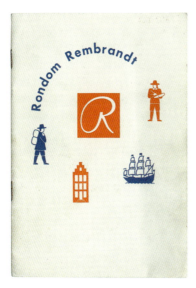

1.51 The cover of the booklet accompanying this exhibition enacts the idea of 'around Rembrandt'. (188 x 132 mm)

the historical background, wars and peace, Rembrandt's contemporaries, the flourishing of the country and of the cities of Amsterdam and Leiden. The same synchronic method could be applied to Rembrandt's private life as to world events, with self-portraits and portraits of those near to him serving as illustration. A large chart with photographs of all the self-portraits introduced our division of his life into four phases: childhood, young manhood, mature manhood, old age, to which we then allocated the colours green, red, blue, brown. The periods of success and of decline in his life were then shown by means of this colour coding; for example, through the number of his pupils in the four periods. Photographs of enlarged details of his paintings showed how his brush strokes altered. This was probably the only presentation that, in its concentration on the pictures, was aimed at the museum visitor; it pleased me that at least one visitor was especially grateful just for this chart.

As a special attraction, Neurath thought up a series of devices with certain questions concerning the exhibition, which could be answered by turning a switch, and then at the end one heard whether the answer was right or wrong. At a subsequent exhibition for De Bijenkorf, 'Het Rollende Rad' [the rolling wheel], this kind of apparatus was even more popular, because with these devices wheels really began to roll. [1.52] Here Neurath used the experience of something we had done already in Vienna. The Städtische Versicherungsanstalt [municipal insurance service] had asked for an exhibition to attract people to the quiet place where they had their office – not even a beautiful fountain helped. So we installed the Zeitschau [time-show], with continually changing presentations of contemporary events, and with a number of devices with which people could test their dexterity or powers of concentration; Neurath had sought advice on their design from the psychologist Ichheiser, who was concerned with ability testing. At midday one had to squeeze into the Zeitschau; the Versicherungsanstalt was satisfied.

During one of Neurath's several visits to New York, the publisher Alfred A. Knopf came to him with the request for an Isotype picture book, and Neurath proposed the present-day world as a theme; he would need a year to produce it. He came home with this good news: we already have so much material for this, we just need to get down to it, he said. Just before we started on the work we had a discussion

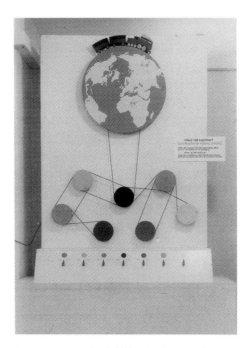

1.52 In 1939 a second exhibition in three copies was made for De Bijenkorf, on the history of the Dutch railways, featuring displays that visitors could set in motion.

about it, and this time it was I who urged: you have been given complete freedom, why not use the opportunity to make something quite new? To bring text and pictures much more intimately together? It was a happy suggestion, and Neurath's powers of creation were set in motion, driving the book – *Modern man in the making* – on from the beginning right to the end. [1.53 –1.54] My transformation responsibilities did not now end just with the graphic presentation, but extended to its arrangement with the text on the page; I was also much involved with the gathering of material. We now just had Arntz for graphic design, which helped the unity of the whole book. But more even than the pleasure in its graphic aspects, the greatest pleasure for me is in the immediacy of Neurath's formulations: his knowledge, his accusations, his wishes and hopes, his worries, his humour and his optimism are still evident in the pictures and text. Close

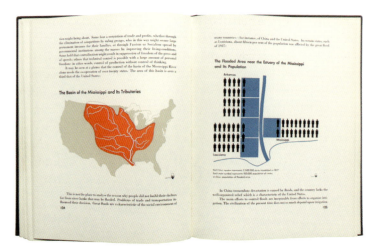

1.53

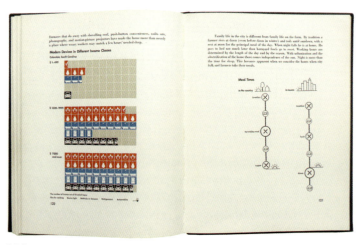

1.54

1.53–1.54 *Modern man in the making* (New York: Knopf, 1939) could be planned page by page, with Otto Neurath writing the text, and the charts – made by the essential team of Neurath, Reidemeister, Arntz – designed to fit just where they were needed. (265 x 210 mm)

collaboration with the publisher was necessary: we had to adapt to the restrictions on the use of colour on each page, and our layout had to be followed exactly by the printer. That happened. *Modern man in the making* appeared in 1939, shortly before the outbreak of war in Europe. It was published in the USA and in Britain, and Dutch and Swedish translations were started immediately. It was the last piece of work that we carried out with our old colleagues. Then the invasion came. At the parting, Neurath said: everyone must decide for themselves now. As foreigners, we were put under house arrest and were thus separated. When the Dutch surrendered, Neurath and I decided to escape, and the two others to stay.

England and Oxford

We arrived in England just as 'enemy aliens' were being interned. Eventually, in February 1941, we were released and were invited to stay in Oxford. The first person who came to us suggesting work together was Paul Rotha, a pioneer of the documentary film. He knew *Modern man in the making* and had heard that Neurath was in England. For a film about blood transfusion he needed diagrams to explain blood groups, and he thought that we could help him. That was the start of some years of good work together. But before we became immersed in the problems of blood transfusion, there was an even more urgent job: the public was to be encouraged to collect certain kinds of waste for reuse. The film *A few ounces a day* used diagrams right the way through. We received a text, and I designed an unbroken sequence of pictures to accompany it. It started at New York: a group of ships were departing over the ocean waves; at the left edge of the picture the skyscrapers disappearing, and also the waves becoming still; an explosion, and a ship sinks. And so it continued, until at the end all the collected ounces refill a ship. In all the other films that we made with Rotha, our diagrams were inserted into the photographic parts, where the argument required it, and thus our collaboration sometimes began already at the first stages of conception. Film animation strengthened the effect of our diagrams.

For example, we showed the distribution of income in England in the following steps: a series of symbols, representing the total population, on a column of coins, representing the total annual income, so that the average income is allotted to everyone. Then: but it is not like that; many have much less – they sink down – only a few have the average, some have more – they rise a bit – and one has very much more – it rises and rises, until it finally comes to a halt. We were once there when this was shown in a cinema and heard the 'ah' of astonishment from the public. For this film work we provided charts for the key positions and gave verbal instructions for how the transitions were to be made. All the intermediate drawings necessary for the animation were done by a special firm. Rotha and Neurath planned to develop the technique of animation themselves in a firm of their own; they also had a plan for the joint production of filmstrips, which were being increasingly used in schools. Nothing came of this.

During the War, as well as the film work, there was soon also book illustration work to do, most of it in our familiar manner. We had already found drawing teachers and some of their pupils to work with us, and we had soon remade our lexicon of symbols, using process-engraved blocks and no longer linocuts. Before getting a small printing press of our own again, we asked a printing company to print the symbols. All the war-time work came through the Ministry of Information. After the War, the production of films and books had to be reorganized. We still did a number of films, for example two for use in schools, about the history of letterforms and the history of printing. The first book job was a visual history of mankind; an international approach had come to be important, and so a visual treatment seemed especially appropriate. It all started with a large committee, from which however Professor Joseph Lauwerys kept in contact with the work. A research assistant gathered piles of material for us, first on the early history of mankind and their discoveries, such as hunting large animals, mining, fire, tools. For some subjects the presentation was achieved through easily understandable sequences of scenes, for example in the case of discovering and making fire. With others, however, I sat helpless in front of the many pages of information and said: I can't make a picture from this. But Neurath just said: of course you can. It concerned life in lake-dwellings built on stilts. [1.55–1.57] What I did was to put the material to one side, to think

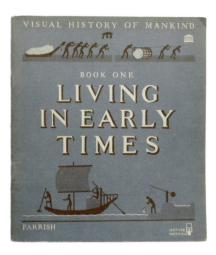

1.55 Cover of the first of the 'Visual history of mankind' series of books: *Living in early times*, London: Max Parrish, 1948. (219 x 194 mm)

back over it, and ask myself: what is especially worth noticing in it? It seemed important to me, then, that the protection that people sought in their lake-dwellings was not from other people, but from wild animals, which could not come near when the bridge was drawn up – something that one could not see in the usual illustrations. That could only be explained by comparison of two pictures: life during day-time, life at night. It was then easy to bring in various other kinds of information, about tools, boats and fishing, hunting and agriculture, cattle and fire-places. This chart had some importance in our discussions with Professor Gordon Childe, whom, together with our publisher Wolfgang Foges, we visited in Edinburgh, in order to show him our work for this book. He said that if we showed this form of village, which was only an exceptional case, we should also show the much more general one, and he gave us documentation about the excavations in Köln-Lindenthal.

I always showed my sketches to Neurath, right to the last, before I gave them for production. If he proposed another approach, it now often happened that I had already tried and rejected it. But if we found that his suggestion was an improvement, he was pleased, he said, that something could still occur to him too. It was however

1.56

1.57

1.56–1.57 A broader, less strictly quantitative approach informs later Isotype work, while developing some of the methods already employed. For example the tabular configuration of the material in the first spread can be seen in earlier work [1.48]. (*Living in early times*)

different with the work on the visual history of mankind: with his extensive historical knowledge and vivid imagination, Neurath came very much to the fore, and I was just his helping hand. He contributed to the graphic details, for example in the plan and elevation of the medieval town. Neurath died when two-thirds of the work was completed. What now?

Rotha came very soon, to say that he wanted the collaboration with the Isotype Institute to carry on as before. Foges also came and said the same thing; he had noticed how Neurath always wanted to discuss everything with me first, before deciding. The board of the Isotype Institute showed the same unquestioning attitude towards me; they were always a group of friends, ready to help. Neurath had thought out the transfer: he had considered us as partners in our contract of employment with the Institute; both of us were Secretaries of the Institute and 'Directors of Studies'; when either of us died, the duties and rights fell to the other. All this was encouraging. I had to carry the work on, and I had to take final responsibilities myself.

Of the many continuing jobs, the completion of the visual history was the hardest. It was some help that we were dealing with historical themes for Rotha (the histories of letterforms and of printing). On the other hand, difficulties arose from dealing with a new man for the book work: Foges enlarged his firm and created his own publishing department, with Max Parrish in charge. Unlike Foges, who had known about us already in Vienna, Parrish had never met Neurath, and our whole approach was foreign to him. I gave him *International picture language* to read, but that did not help; he said only that it was utopian. Our views on many things were essentially different, and with this lack of harmony, nothing happened quite as I had wanted it. Joseph Lauwerys was always available for advice over the choice of subjects for the charts still to be done in the second and third books, and we managed it in the end. I did not want to bother Gordon Childe with this, though he was now in London. I asked him just to look over all the work at the end, before it went to the printer. He also stayed in touch with me afterwards.

London

With new projects of book series and magazines, Foges had so much urgent work for us that he asked me to come to London with the Institute and offered us space in a large building that he had moved into. Meanwhile I had succeeded in designing a children's book that attracted the interest of Max Parrish: now we've got something, he said. Neurath had planned two already: 'Tits for tots' and 'Just boxes'. I took up the second; it played with the idea that boxes which look similar from the outside are inside quite different: jack-in-a-boxes, cameras, radios, etc. But one then got on to things that were too difficult, and so it was not yet satisfactory. I avoided this by giving up the similarity of outer form: so I could take a wasp's nest and a lighthouse, volcano and cave with stalactites. A similar book followed, and then one about London Underground trains, for which all the information we wanted was helpfully provided by the management. I had a great struggle with Parrish about the representation of Piccadilly Circus Station: he wanted something done in perspective, so that one could see the real angles at which two lines crossed; I explained that I would then lose any possibility of explaining the

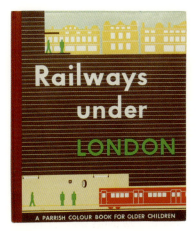

1.58

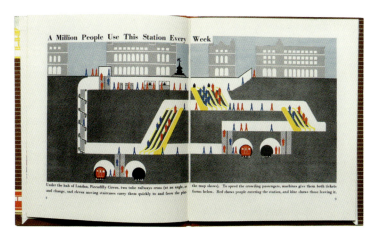

1.59

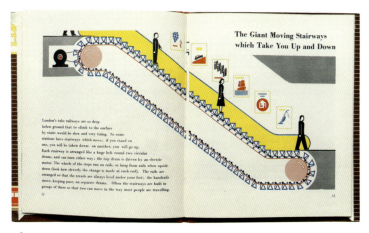

1.60

1.58–1.60 Isotype principles of visual clarity and consistency could also be applied to a straightforward explanation of 'how things work'. Marie Neurath, *Railways under London*, London: Max Parrish, 1948. (223 x 192 mm)

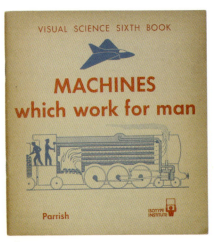

1.61

process of changing trains. It was a matter of the fundamentals of our method and this time I could not concede. [1.58–1.60] The book was a success. It led to the firm of Cable & Wireless coming to Parrish with the request that we make a book about their technical processes: enquiries often came from schools and they had no appropriate material. We got mountains of information; it was difficult, but worth doing. I learned to master the technical processes, analysing them down into their smallest parts and showing side by side what was simultaneous. The children's books continued, and especially so after it was decided to do a series on nature, as well as the technical series. Another series of school books was also produced: 'Visual science'. [1.61–1.63] It was essentially easier for me than the history book, because it dealt with the natural sciences, which I had once studied.

After the publication of the 'Visual history of mankind', a publisher of filmstrips (Common Ground) came asking us to make filmstrips for him. Discussions started, then a contract and years of productive and friendly collaboration. We adapted to the production requirements in making our pictures, and also the choice of subjects was jointly agreed. We were asked for historical themes most of all. I got down to making an adaptation of the first volume of our 'Visual history'. I had to immerse myself in this new medium: much less

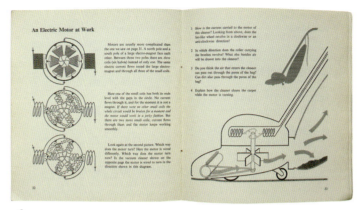

1.62

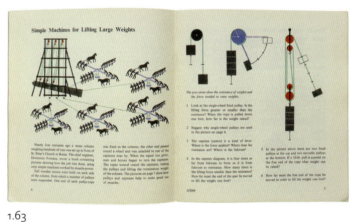

1.63

1.61–1.63 The science to be explained here is intrinsically visual: the diagrams follow the material, with the help of colour coding. *Machines which work for man*, London: Max Parrish, 1952. (215 x 202 mm)

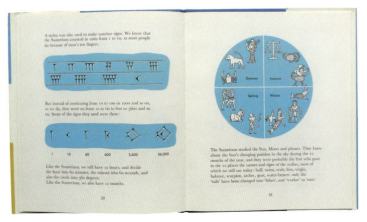

1.64

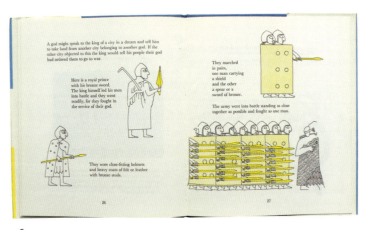

1.65

1.64–1.66 In a later series of books, the visual style of the culture being presented was used. Marie Neurath & Evelyn Worboys, *They lived like this in ancient Mesopotamia*, London: Max Parrish, 1964. (213 x 185 mm)

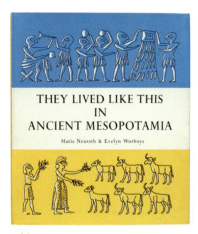

1.66

should be put into one frame than into the page of a book. On the other hand, one is freer in the choice of colours and can also include photographic material. We treated many ancient cultures: Mesopotamia and Egypt, Greece and Rome, Palestine, the world religions, and so on. The subjects fascinated me. This started already with the Mesopotamian cylindrical seals and their meaning. Before I delivered our pictures to the filmstrip publisher, I showed them to Max Parrish, proposing a book about this. Before he had come to any decision, he was dismissed by his board. There followed an interlude that was very useful for me, with the publishers Heinemann, where the children's books editor radically shortened my text. Then I went back to the successor of Max Parrish, and a series of twenty books, 'They lived like this', was published under his direction. [1.64–1.66] Complete freedom was given to me and I enjoyed this work. We showed how people lived through their own means of representation: cylindrical seals and Egyptian wall-pictures; Greek and Cretan vase pictures; Chinese, Japanese, Mexican forms were introduced as means, and the word art never appeared. Only occasionally were there Isotype presentations, in the narrow sense, but all the pictures had to be read in conjunction with the text.

West Africa

In the 1950s I had one quite special experience. Through Foges, I came into contact with Nigeria. One morning he brought me a booklet by the Prime Minister of Western Nigeria and asked me to read it quickly and to present its main ideas in visual form; the man was coming at 3 o'clock that afternoon, and I should come too. So I was there when Awolowo looked at my sketches and discussed with his private secretary how one could best use something like this, perhaps as leaflets to be scattered by aircraft. Then I received an invitation to come for six months to Ibadan; I asked for two shorter stays rather than this. I had received already in London a document about the introduction of compulsory school attendance, and designed a chart from it. When I then walked around the streets and markets of Ibadan, I thought: why should these people struggle with my chart, and threw it away. Instead of this I designed a pictorial booklet of 16 pages, developing the argument step by step. [1.67–1.70] And there were further subjects to be treated: agriculture, health, the budget.

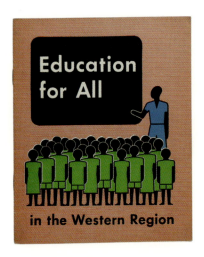

1.67 Cover of *Education for all in the Western Region*, [Ibadan]: Western Regional Government, 1955. (202 x 166 mm)

I was sent to the hospital at Ibadan and also to medical stations in the country and to a lepers' colony. A doctor in the hospital showed me the crowd in the waiting room and complained that the same patients come again and again, because they always make the same mistakes. I suggested special pictorial broadsheets, for the walls of waiting rooms and elsewhere, and the Minister of Health agreed at once. When I came to Western Nigeria for the second time, I was able to bring proofs of some booklets with me and to try them out. I went to a school that I had pleasant memories of, from earlier visits, and asked the head-teacher if the 25 copies that I had brought could be distributed to the class. I saw with pleasure how the children eagerly examined the pictures. When the teacher interrupted this and asked a pupil to read the text aloud, I was rather disturbed; I suggested that I should rather come back the next day and asked him to look through the booklet before then. That proved itself in an extraordinary way; now the text and pictures were read together, and the teacher explained to the children what exports are, with a drawing on the blackboard: the coast-line of the country, the sea indicated by wavy lines, a ship leaving with a cargo – the Isotype method, fully

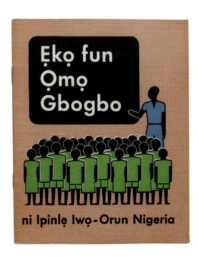

1.68 Cover of the Yoruba edition of *Education for all in the Western Region*.

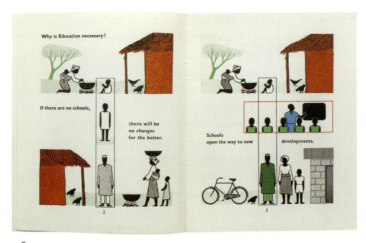

1.69

1.70

1.69–1.70 The visual statement here is of step-by-step development and comparison: the argument is left to the viewer to discover and consider. (English and Yoruba editions of *Education for all in the Western Region*)

comprehended. Of course the symbols had to 'speak' to the Nigerians, just as they had to the Viennese; men, women, children had to look as they did there; houses could not have chimneys; but in the essential rules of transformation, nothing needed to be changed. Our booklets also found success among educated circles there, as was later told to me by Rotimi Williams, the Minister for Local Government, at a reception in London; he also thought that the particularly high turn-out in elections in Western Nigeria was due to our booklet explaining voting procedures. For a time there was a plan to instruct a group of Nigerians in our methods; but although I did everything in preparation for it, I was not really confident.

Looking to the future

We were not even able to provide for the continuation of our Institute in England, in spite of various attempts to do this – I can remember three of them still in Neurath's lifetime. The most hopeful one was probably that in connection with the work for the housing programme in Bilston; a town-council would again have provided the basis. There were further plans after Neurath's death; I also tried to introduce a successor into my work. Nothing succeeded.

My last job was a filmstrip about the history of medicine. The publisher was pleased when he heard that I was working on this subject, because he had nothing on it. Then suddenly he had lost his life in a road accident. That also meant a tragic and sudden end for my work with them; I had only an introductory meeting with the successors; it removed all incentive to go on with the collaboration. The same thing happened with the book publisher; there was a reorganization, and I had to deal with people whose values had nothing in common with ours. I was now over 70 years old and I decided to bring the work to a close. So it had a real end, just as it had a very clear beginning.

There was now only one more task: to find a resting home for all our material, so that it could be of use to younger generations. This happened through a lucky accident. Two students telephoned me from Reading and requested an interview. I was astonished by the kind of questions that they put to me: what appeared fundamental to them was also what is fundamental to me. I asked about their work and their teacher and so heard about Michael Twyman. At my request he soon came to visit me. That was the first step towards our contract with the University of Reading. Our material was taken there when I gave up the office. In 1975 an exhibition about Isotype was made at Reading, and afterwards Robin Kinross wrote his postgraduate thesis on Otto Neurath's contribution to visual communication. And elsewhere in the world there are people for whom our work means something. I have written this sketch for them.

2

The work of the transformer

Marie Neurath once described the work of the group making the charts at the Gesellschafts- und Wirtschaftsmuseum.[1]

> During the years in Vienna the team in our workshop usually consisted of the director, two transformers, two chief artists, and a number of technicians skilled in the work process. Among the scholars whom Neurath called in for their advice and research were experts in statistics, history, medicine, cartography, geography, engineering, industrial management, history of art, etc.
>
> This is how the team worked (except when we had to make charts for some special exhibition): an idea was formed by Neurath; he discussed it with an expert to have his idea checked and to get suitable material. The transformer was present at such discussions, to get acquainted with the subject. The transformer then took over the material and developed the way to present it visually. The sketch (in pencil and colour pencils) was discussed with Neurath (and sometimes the expert) until a final rough was agreed upon; this was copied into a duplicate book, and the coloured top copy handed to the artist who took charge of design and finished artwork, in constant contact with Neurath and the transformer.

She also explained the process that they called transformation:

> From the data given in words and figures a way has to be found to extract the essential facts and put them into picture form. It is the

---

1. The two quotations that follow come from Marie Neurath's article 'Isotype', in *Instructional Science*, vol. 3, no. 2, 1974, at p. 137 and p. 136. I have edited her text very slightly, to let it fit better into this context. Another of Marie Neurath's retrospective articles ('Otto Neurath and Isotype', *Graphic Design* [Japan], no. 42, 1971, pp. 11–30) is useful in its annotation of some early charts.

responsibility of the 'transformer' to understand the data, to get all necessary information from the expert, to decide what is worth transmitting to the public, how to make it understandable, how to link it with general knowledge or with information already given in other charts. In this sense, the transformer is the trustee of the public. He has to remember the rules and to keep them, adding new variations where advisable, at the same time avoiding unnecessary deviations which would only confuse. He has to produce a rough of the chart in which many details have been decided: title; arrangement, type, number and colour of symbols; caption, etc. It is a blueprint from which the artist works.

The idea of transformation, and some of the principles and methods of Isotype, could be fully examined by looking at all the materials of the work: the raw data supplied or gathered, the trials and rough sketches, the final layout made by the transformer, as well as the finished result. For the work done after 1941, the materials for such an investigation can sometimes be found in the archive at Reading. For the present discussion it may be enough to look just at the finished results, with the help of some thoughts added by the principal transformer, Marie Neurath.[2]

An early chart

This chart [2.01], made in 1925, was among the earliest productions of the Gesellschafts- und Wirtschaftsmuseum in Wien, and it has sometimes been cited in order to show how primitive were the

2. Much of the rest of this chapter is drawn from an article that I published in 1982, which incorporated comments by Marie Neurath: 'Isotype: die Aufgabe der Transformation', in: F. Stadler (ed.), *Arbeiterbildung in der Zwischenkriegszeit*, Vienna: Löcker Verlag, 1982, pp. 189–97. I have used my original English text and translated into English the 'interventions' that I asked Marie Neurath to add to it.
3. Otto Neurath, 'Schwarzweissgraphic', ÖGZ, Jg. 3, Nr. 10, 15 May 1926 (GBS, p. 51).

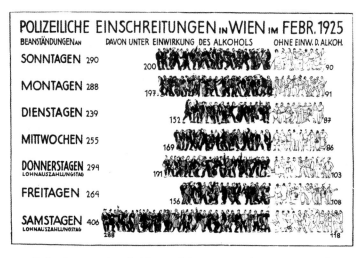

2.01 Police interventions in Vienna, February 1925. (ÖGZ, 15.05.1926)

beginnings of Isotype. The first published critique of the chart was made by Otto Neurath. In an article in the *Österreichische Gemeinde Zeitung* (15 May 1926) he wrote as follows:

> This sort of livening-up detracts from the real theme of the chart: one becomes more interested in the individual cases than in the statistical relations. Because one does not know the individual cases of arrest, this says more than one knows. If one knows nothing except 'arrests under the influence of alcohol', one must make just one type for it and repeat that, as often as the statistical information demands. There was at first a certain timidity to be overcome, before being able to repeat.[3]

And one could add that it is also a kind of 'timidity' to put the exact figures as part of the visual display; this was soon given up.

One can certainly make objections against the symbols of this chart, and it is characteristic of Otto Neurath's essentially critical attitude that he was the first to make them. But in the larger matter of transformation, there is evidence here of a surprisingly developed approach.

Already in one of the first charts, information runs to and from a central axis (perhaps inspired by 'population tree' bar charts: see 1.08, p. 17 above). Axial configurations came to be frequently used in Isotype work. A simple approach would have been to employ simple rows, each starting from a constant vertical alignment on the left. Configuration around a central axis allows comparisons to be made both within and between the two categories of those under the influence and those not under the influence of alcohol.

Another aspect of the configuration should be noticed. The rows are arranged in a natural order: not in order of magnitude, but by sequence of the days of the week. The information can thus better speak for itself, although a particular interpretation is suggested to the viewer by the noting of the 'Lohnauszahlungstag': wages are paid on Thursdays and Saturdays. This principle of finding an order that allows (and does not force) significance to become visually evident is one that informs all the best Isotype work.

[MN writes:] I am glad to read again this early remark, from 1926 – I had forgotten it. At the start, Neurath's self-criticism was indeed the only thing that lead to further development. One can hardly see any way to count the figures through this disorderliness, even if it does follow from the nature of the subject. In the later charts, when the symbols stood next to each other in good sobriety, people said it looked military. It is hard to say much about that: it's part of the bargain.

Indeed, arrangement according to size creates a boring sameness in a chart: nothing apart from a decline in numbers. With this also the main interest is diverted from the picture to the text. But wouldn't our decision to find general rules of arrangement, and not be governed by the content of the chart itself, be better illustrated by another example; for example, by a chart in which a geographically determined sequence of countries is used? I do not know any examples in which chronological sequence is sacrificed to order of size (not in Isotype, nor elsewhere).

Charts on births and deaths

Marie Neurath refers (p. 14 above) to the working out of some of the conventions of Isotype. The changes of approach that are evident in successive births and deaths charts show the adoption of the idea of using the conventional Western reading pattern: from left to right and top to bottom.

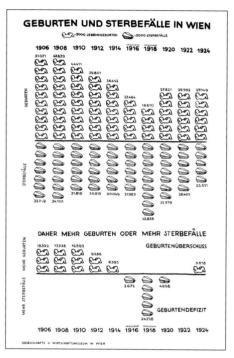

2.02 Births and deaths in Vienna. (T3c, ÖGZ, 15.05.1926)

This chart [2.02], which seems to have been drawn entirely by hand, must date from the first year of work, 1925. The chart is in two parts: above, all the information is given, then below the conclusion is stated explicitly ('Thus more births or more deaths: excess of births / excess of deaths'). Although the symbols represent a stated unit quantity, the exact figures are added too.

81

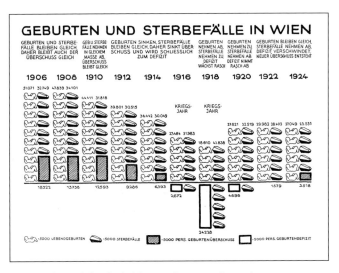

2.03 Births and deaths in Vienna. (ÖGZ, 15.08.1925)

Published in 1925, this variant [2.03] shows another rather didactic approach. A commentary on the information runs above the columns, and the excess of births and deaths in the war period is emphasized with the box shape by the side of the death symbols: they were not left to speak for themselves.

Here [2.04] the excess of births and deaths is spelled out with an added sign, although this is done more subtly than in the previous example. Gravestones now replace coffins. As Marie Neurath explains (p. 14 above), this avoids the suggestion that the coffins were the size of babies.

Here [2.05] the positive indication of excess births and deaths is no longer used: viewers are allowed to see this for themselves. The symbols for both categories have been refined.

The configuration is now switched [2.06], to use the top-to-bottom, left-to-right convention that became normative in Isotype work.

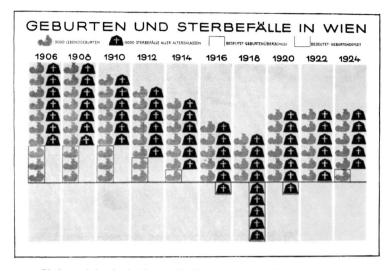

2.04 Births and deaths in Vienna. (T3f, ÖGZ, 15.05.1926)

2.05 War and population increase in Austria. (T3d)

2.06 Births and deaths in Germany. (DBW, p. 43)

These symbols, and perhaps those in the previous chart, would have been designed by Gerd Arntz.

This succession of charts is typical of the progress of the work in its first few years. The essential principle of repeating units rather than enlarging them is there right from the start, at the beginning of 1925. However there follows a restless, evidently self-critical process of experiment and variation: in the principles of arrangement, more especially in the drawing of the symbols, and most especially in the more peripheral features of treatment of titles and explanations of exactly what the presentation means.

Charts on unemployment

These charts would have been made for showing at the Gesundheitshaus in Berlin-Kreuzberg, under the arrangement between the Gesellschafts- und Wirtschaftsmuseum and the mayor of the district (see Marie Neurath's description, p. 45 above). On the evidence of the last dates that they show, one can give the years in which they were made: 1929, 1931, and 1932. Because they can be so precisely dated and because they treat the same subject, they offer useful points of reference in following the development of Isotype in these years, which one can see as its first period of maturity. Although it must be said that, with just a single varying element, these charts are less interesting than those (more characteristic of Isotype) that provide a comparison between two or more varying elements. (The third chart of the series does introduce a differentiation within the single category of 'unemployed' – between those receiving unemployment insurance payments, or 'crisis benefits', and those doing welfare work – though this is not visible in black and white.)

The first chart of this series [2.07] is one of the earliest to show what became the standard Isotype symbol for an unemployed person. It is also among the first charts in which symbols are marked off into easily countable groups. This was only possible when the symbols had become properly modular: with the capacity for repetition, combina-

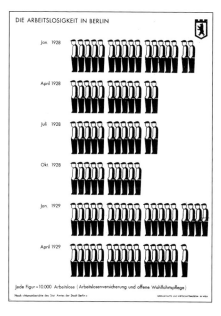

2.07 Unemployment in Berlin. (T104a)

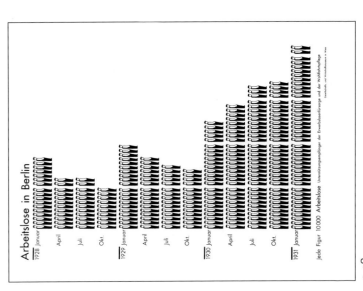

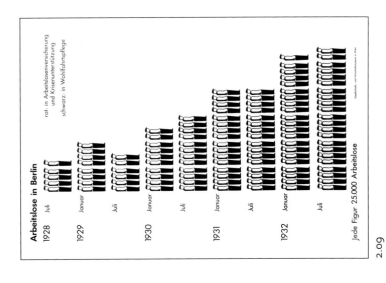

2.08–2.09 Unemployed in Berlin. (T104b / T8006)

86

tion, division (fractioning), and the capacity to exist in balance with other symbols – all in a visually satisfactory way. This development of modular symbols began to be achieved when, at the end of 1928, Gerd Arntz became a member of the Gesellschafts- und Wirtschafts-museum. Arntz's contribution was to enable the realization of what had obviously been striven for, but only imperfectly achieved.

In the second example [2.08], the number of unemployed – and of symbols – is much greater, and the chart itself must have been of a larger size than the first one. The groups are now composed of ten symbols; to group these longer lines in fives would have broken them up too much.

This problem was made more acute in the third 'edition' of this chart [2.09] – and it was tackled by changing the unit of representation. To correspond to the new unit of 1:25,000, the symbols are now grouped in fours. (Groups of five or ten would not be meaningful here.) The gap between groups seems – certainly at this scale of re-duction – slightly too narrow: it is not emphatically different enough from the normal distance between the symbols. The adjustment needed would be a matter of millimetres. Fine visual decisions of this kind would occur in every chart: no system, no method, can solve them once and for all.

Perhaps the most interesting thing in these three charts, from the point of view of design or transformation, is the decision concern-ing the direction in which the symbols face. The rationale for the left-facing symbols of the first chart would be that those joining the 'queue', with each new row, join at the end of it – as they would do in reality. In the second and third charts, this idea is discarded in favour of the general rule that symbols follow reading direction, from left to right. There is clearly a balance of alternatives here, each with merits of its own; it is not a matter of following some simple set of rules.

   This series of charts also, incidentally, provides illustration of the refinement that was developed in the more peripheral aspects of design. The titles of the chart was set first all in capitals, then in capi-tals and small letters; first in medium-weight type, then in bold. One can see increasing care taken in the typographic treatment of the years and months on the left side of the chart.

[MN:] I have to say that the direction in which the unemployed face does not really matter to me, and it seems to have little effect on the intelligibility of the chart. As also with the 'births and deaths' charts, we hesitated: should the excess of deaths or births be shown on the left or the right? I know what I prefer, personally; but my arguments are so weak that they can be overruled.

What strikes me as of greater importance in these charts about unemployment is that they say that, in the general crisis, seasonal variations disappeared. This is most evident in the second chart. In the third chart I suspect that, probably for reasons of space, we left out the figures for January 1928.

Charts on agriculture and industry

Other principles of configuring material can be seen in charts on agriculture and industry in Germany that were sometimes shown together, as a pair. One can follow developments in treatment of the two sets of material from their first publication in 1927 to last versions in 1930.

For 'Betriebsgrößen in der Landwirtschaft 1925' [2.10], a 'chessboard' configuration was used (this was Neurath's term). The total agricultural land of Germany is shown, divided according to the different systems of farming. Each unit represents a certain area of land (1 million hectares) and not a percentage figure. As always in Isotype –and this is characteristic of *all* of Neurath's work–information is stated in the most concrete and direct form: abstracted units, such as percentages, are avoided. Others who have made pictorial statistics do not seem to be as sensitive to this question: one can find clear and concrete images that turn out to be representing mathematical constructs.

Although this chart has a definitive character, the way in which the material is disposed on the 'chessboard' is not obvious. The unit of representation had to be chosen. The simple ratio of 1:1 million hectares gives the 25 units that would form a square of 5 x 5 units

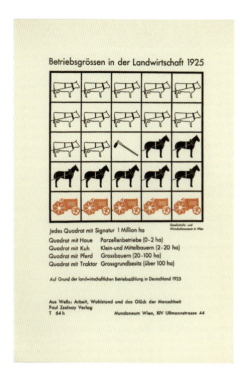

2.10 Size of working unit in the agricultural economy of Germany, 1925. (Source as for 1.31)

—this was a piece of luck. What might seem to be the obvious rule for ordering the sequence of the unit squares (start with the smallest owners and proceed to the largest) was not followed. Instead the material was divided into its two major parts, of equal size, and these are balanced against each other—and the remaining, exceptional item (smallholdings) is placed in the central position. This has the effect of giving visual prominence to the 'remainder'. Perhaps this can be justified only if the intention is indeed (as is implied visually) to consider smallholdings—land that provides only for those who cultivate it—as not simply the smallest agricultural category, but rather as a unique category and worth drawing attention to.

   The drawing of the symbols plays a part here. The cow, horse, and tractor, have approximately equal visual weight. But this visual

89

2.11 Size of working unit in the agricultural economy of Germany, 1925. (T64h)

equality is upset by showing the cow in outline, while the two symbols for the large concerns are fully coloured (that is, they are black). The hoe is clearly differentiated from the other symbols by its much lighter visual weight and by its striking diagonal position. The intention does clearly seem to be to distinguish the category of smallholding as an exception, through this identifying symbol, as well as through its special position.

It is interesting to look at earlier versions of this chart. [2.11, 2.12] These were published in 1927 and 1929, while the final version was published around 1930.[4] Evidently the configuration of the material could not be improved upon. The drawing of the symbols does show a process of refinement and intelligent simplification. Perhaps the

---

4. Stylistically this last version of 'Betriebsgrössen in der Landwirtschaft 1925' could have fitted into *Gesellschaft und Wirtschaft*, published in 1930, yet it was not published there, although its partner chart 'Die Beschäftigten in den Gewerbebetrieben des Deutschen Reiches' was [2.13].

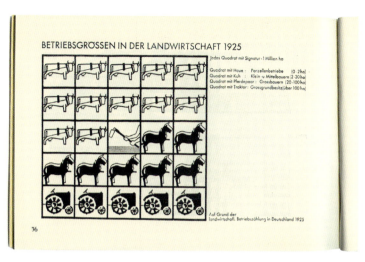

2.12 Size of working unit in the agricultural economy of Germany, 1925. (DBW, p. 36)

most striking change is in the hoe symbol: especially the changes in the visual effects of its backgrounds. In each case these serve to make it look the exceptional item.

'Die Beschäftigten in den Gewerbebetrieben des Deutschen Reiches' [2.13] shows a comparison between the data for two different years. (One wonders why such a comparison could not also be made in the agricultural chart.) 'Führungsbilder' are used here to distinguish the three categories of small, medium, and large concerns. By this time, these 'visual headings' had become a standard device in Isotype charts.

The most interesting aspect of the transformation in this chart is the way in which the symbols are placed, so that comparisons can be made within each group and between the two groups. The 'axial' principle of arrangement is used; this means that the symbols of the left and right categories in the two groups extend from the same axis. The second group is made up of 20 units, which, fortunately, can form two rows of 10, with the right internal composition (so that exact internal alignment of the rows is established). So in both of these charts, the material fell into place happily, and no use was made of percentages.

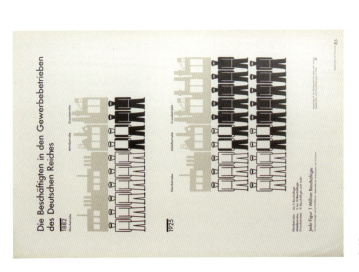

2.13 Workers in commercial enterprises in Germany. (T64f)
2.14 Small, medium and large enterprises in German industry (T64a)

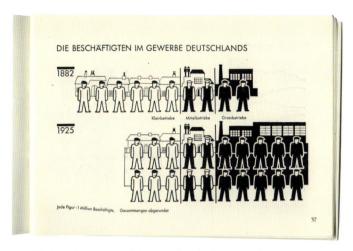

2.15 Workers in commercial enterprises in Germany. (DBW, p. 37)

[MN:] I am surprised to read that in the agriculture chart the smallholdings seem so important. If I remember correctly, this was not intentional. For the transformation, this 'group of one' was indeed welcome as a hole-filler. We did indeed have to work to form rows of five units, in order to achieve a closed and in fact square form. It was lucky that there was a subgroup of five units.

We could have decided to separate the smallholdings. Then we would have got four rows of six units for the other kinds of agriculture, with the division into two halves that RK mentioned, and put the single square of the smallholdings above. The sequence of small to larger land-holdings would then have been maintained. With the arrangement as a square, we had to give up any exclusive focus on increasing visual weight in the symbols.

Luck often played a part; it helped in the industries chart. The luck was that in 1925 there were 20 million employed; then we looked for a year in which there were 10 million. The arrangement in rows of ten allows the doubling to be easily seen, but at the same time one sees the subdivisions – the percentages. One can see, for example, that those employed in small businesses have remained the same in absolute numbers, but have fallen from six in

93

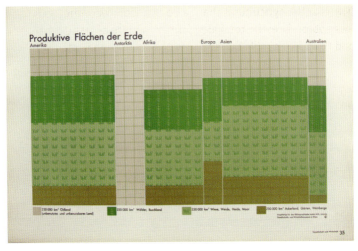

2.16 The earth's productive land. (GUW, chart 35)

every ten to three in every ten. The real piece of luck in this chart is that the middle group has doubled in absolute terms and thus remained the same in percentage terms; so there are two continuous vertical axes, and the shift in the two groups on either size of the central part is clearly visible.

It is worth looking at an earlier version of this chart [2.14], which throws some light on the approach eventually arrived at. This chart was published (along with 2.11) in a booklet of 1928, *Entwicklung von Landwirtschaft und Gewerbe in Deutschland*. Here each symbol represents half a million employed people; so there are twice as many symbols as in the later chart (where each symbol is 1 million employed). And in this earlier chart a middle point in the development is represented: here are figures for 1907, later cut in the interests of clarity and making a strong point. A further version [2.15], published in 1929, shows the final configuration used. The development from the chart of 1929 to that of 1930 [2.13] is in the drawing of the symbols and the 'Führungsbilder', which are moved from an overall background element to being strictly headings.

[MN:] For the agricultural chart, a comparison over time would be less appropriate; the total area farmed is more or less unchanged, and there is probably hardly any noticeable change in the subdivisions.

There are quite a number of Isotype charts that use percentages; for example, how many out of every ten babies reach the age of 70; how many out of every ten people live in towns and in the country. Also, for example, in the charts about infant mortality, we show percentages. But we showed this very concretely: the number of deaths and also a hundred infants as a group in the background. There is also a series of charts in which absolute and percentage data is shown in combination: population in a city and in the country at different times, or in different countries; world empires; land use. With land use, for example, percentage division shows the character of the landscape, and the absolute sizes allow us comparison and overview of arable land, woodland, and so on. [2.16] But in these charts we gave the absolute numbers in the explanation of the symbols. We did not need to speak of percentages; we could show them concretely.

1. The first section of this chapter derives from a part of my introduction to GBS; the second section is developed from my article 'On the influence of Isotype', *Information Design Journal*, vol. 2, no. 2, 1981, pp. 122–30; the third section is freshly written.

2. 'From hieroglyphics to Isotype', *Future Books*, vol. 3, 1946, pp. 93–100 (GBS, pp. 636–45).

3. Principal sources for the history of graphic statistics are: H. Gray Funkhouser, 'Historical development of the graphical representation of statistical data', *Osiris*, vol. 3, no. 1, 1937, pp. 269–404; James R. Beniger & Dorothy L. Robyn, 'Quantitative graphics in statistics: a brief history', *American Statistician*, vol. 32, no. 1, 1978, pp. 1–11; and in the sequence of books by Edward R. Tufte, most especially his first: *The visual display of quantative information*, Cheshire, CT: Graphics Press, 1983. See also the unpublished dissertation by Patricia Costigan-Eaves: 'Data graphics in the 20th century: a comparative and analytic survey', Rutgers, State University of New Jersey, 1984.

4. This distinction between scientific and popular seems to lie behind Edward Tufte's lack of interest in Isotype. Only in his third book on graphic presentation of information does 'isotype' (he uses the word adjectivally, uncapitalized) make a fleeting appearance. A piece of 'info-graphics' (Tufte's quotation marks – he writes 'the language is as ghastly as the charts') is shown to illustrate 'how pop journalism might depict Snow's work, complete with celebrity factoids, over-compressed data, and the isotype styling of those little coffins' (*Visual explanations*, Cheshire, CT: Graphics Press, 1997, p. 37). 'Over-compressed data' seems to be a principal reason for Tufte's implicit rejection of Isotype. This was confirmed in a letter he wrote me (18 August 1984), after his first book, *The visual display of quantitative information* had been published. I had suggested to him that Isotype belonged in the pantheon of graphic information, along with William Playfair and E.J. Marey. He said that while he liked the design and the politics of Isotype work, he did not like their statistics or 'quantitative depth'.

3

Lessons of Isotype

Isotype and visual traditions

Isotype can be placed within two historical traditions.[1] It may be seen within the development of the graphic presentation of statistics: a lineage that started in the late eighteenth century and which began to flourish in the nineteenth century. The other tradition is the very long one of the communication of information of all kinds for secular, educational purposes, through pictures, diagrams, maps, and other visual means. As well as extending back to ancient times, this larger tradition of visual communication extends across human cultures; while graphic statistics has been an essentially European and North American phenomenon, Neurath himself saw Isotype in the long perspective of human visual communication, as his 'visual autobiography' (in the text published as 'From hieroglyphics to Isotype') makes clear.[2]

Much of the history of these two traditions remains to be discovered. In the development of graphic statistics, we know some of the landmarks, but there remains what must be a mass of relevant books and more or less ephemeral material still buried in libraries and archives. The larger tradition, because of its duration and cultural spread, requires historians with encyclopedic interests (such as Otto Neurath himself). And, in general, the history of graphic communication (that is, outside the areas of the fine and the decorative arts) has suffered from what seems to be a deeply ingrained academic indifference. Any history of graphic statistics or of the larger subject of graphic communication must necessarily be tentative; and, in any case, only a brief sketch is possible here. Nevertheless this sketch will at least propose the historical streams in which Isotype lies.

The founding father of the graphic presentation of statistics is generally acknowledged to be William Playfair (1759–1823), a Scotsman of diverse interests, who published a number of works – especially *The commercial and political atlas* (1786) and *The statistical breviary*

(1801)–in which graphs and other visual means were employed, apparently for the first time, to present economic and social data.[3] If Playfair was an isolated forerunner, later in the nineteenth century two factors combined to make possible the widespread appearance of graphic statistics: the growth of statistics as a means of investigation and knowledge, and the increased spread of pictorial images, made possible by new techniques in printing, providing both entertainment and education for the newly emerging mass readership. It would thus seem obvious that graphic methods should have been developed to present the statistics that were by the end of the last century being gathered on every conceivable topic.

Two kinds of graphic statistics can be distinguished, both for this earlier period and (more clearly) for the recent past and the present: graphic presentations that are intended to help specialist statisticians analyse their data, and those that are intended to help a wide general public understand otherwise forbidding quantified information. Isotype belongs very consciously to the second category: the aim of wide comprehensibility underlies the decision to use pictorial symbols, rather than non-iconic graphic means.[4]

By the end of the nineteenth century, pictorial graphic statistics were coming to be used widely: they can be found in newspapers and journals (though no systematic survey has been attempted) and can be seen in certain less ephemeral publications. One may suspect that an influential figure here was Michael G. Mulhall (1836–1900), who published a number of statistical compilations–notably the *Dictionary of statistics* (1883, and several later editions)–containing some graphic and especially pictorial presentations of selected data.

Mulhall's pictorial statistics [3.01] provide good examples of the kind of work that Neurath criticized and in opposition to which he proposed Isotype. Mulhall's symbols are enlarged in size according to the quantities that they represent; also they are usually ordered in sequence of magnitude, rather than some more natural and useful principle (such as an order derived from geographical location).

3. See page 96.
4. See page 96.

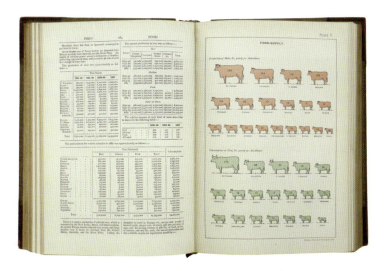

3.01 Mulhall's diagrams are illustrations of his data, rather than transformations of it. As well as the difficulty of not knowing what quantities the pictures actually show, the presentation remains inert in using magnitude as its ordering principle, and in making no effort to compare the two sets of data visually. Michael G. Mulhall, *The dictionary of statistics*, London: George Routledge, 1892. (258 x 195 mm)

Another landmark in this history came with the publication of Willard C. Brinton's *Graphic methods for presenting facts* (1914). This is a long and exhaustive survey of the whole field, and it has been cited as predating Neurath's use of the principle of repeating (rather than enlarging) pictorial symbols to represent quantities.[5] Brinton does indeed show this in one of his many illustrations (p. 39), though his

---

5. See, for example: Herbert Koberstein, '"Wiener Methode der Bildstatistik" und "International System of Typographic Picture Education" (Isotype): informative Graphik und bildhafte Pädagogik', unpublished dissertation, University of Hamburg, 1969, p. 29. In a development of this dissertation, Koberstein went on to put forward his own method of pictorial statistics, based on an ahistorical reduction of Isotype: *Statistik in Bildern: eine graphisch-statistische Darstellungslehre*, C.E. Poeschel Verlag: Stuttgart, 1973. The assumption that Brinton influenced Neurath's method was one of the accusations by Clive Chizlett in an attack on Neurath and Isotype:

example is a crude one, having no clear concept of the unit symbol. But this single example cannot begin to compare with system of Isotype, as refined and developed over many years of work. As regards the question of precedence, it seems unlikely that Neurath would have seen Brinton's book in Vienna when he started the housing museum there in the early 1920s. Even less could he have seen *Graphic methods for presenting facts* around 1917, at the time of his first exploration of visual display at the war-economy museum in Leipzig.[6]

[continued from page 99]
'Damned lies, and statistics: Otto Neurath and Soviet propaganda in the 1930s', *Visible Language*, vol. 26, no. 3/4, pp. 299–321. I responded to this with 'Blind eyes, innuendo and the politics of design: a reply to Clive Chizlett', *Visible Language*, vol. 28, no. 1, pp. 68–79. More recently the idea that Neurath borrowed from Brinton was assumed by Nader Vossoughian in his *Otto Neurath: the language of the global polis* (2008)–with no evidence given for it. A copy of *Graphic methods for presenting facts* was in the library of the Isotype Institute, acquired presumably some time after the emigration to Britain in 1940. Brinton went on to publish another book, *Graphic presentation* (New York: Brinton Associates, 1939). This collects together material he had acquired following the publication of his first book. It is curious that he makes no mention of Isotype, which by that time should certainly have been known to him.
6. Almost nothing is known about the work in Leipzig, but Wolfgang Schumann, who was working in the city and knew Neurath then, remembered: 'Models and charts were in the making. This was the beginning of the activities of visualization which Neurath continued and fully developed in his Social and Economic Museum in Vienna.' (EAS, p. 16.)
7. Neurath's text was unfinished at his death and its intending publisher then brought out another book to replace it: Lancelot Hogben, *From cave painting to comic strip*, London: Parrish, 1949. Hogben's book still has its uses as an exploration of this enormous field.
8. For a good example of a specialized history, see: Arthur H. Robinson, *Early thematic mapping in the history of cartography*, Chicago: University of Chicago Press, 1982.
9. A good deal of this material was kept in the Netherlands during the war and, together with material collected after the emigration of 1940, is now in the Otto and Marie Neurath Isotype Collection, University of Reading. For an instance of direct reference by Neurath to this visual tradition, see IPL, p. 107.

As research discovers other 'proto-Isotype' work that Neurath could have been more likely to have seen, then consideration of Brinton as having a possible direct bearing on Isotype methods will be less necessary. [3.02–3.03] But Brinton's *Graphic methods* remains important testimony to the quantity and diversity of graphic information being produced by that time. The question of any direct predecessor for the founding graphic principle of Isotype should also be considered in the light of the abundance of bad – unclear, inconsistent – pictorial statistics and Neurath's inclination to consistency in graphic presentation, by his own account (in the 'visual autobiography') retained from childhood. One may also remark here that while Neurath was abreast of the concerns of his time – in his visual work as in other things – he was also remarkably independent and in fact unorthodox in his thought, and was helped in this by his wide historical knowledge. He was free from any close dependence on the ideas of his peers and immediate predecessors.

This leads on to the larger tradition in which Isotype may be placed: the history of the graphic communication of information of all kinds. Here the best starting point is Neurath's 'visual autobiography'.[7] The subject has as yet found no generally acknowledged historian, though the growing number of specialist contributions suggests the possibility of a serious synthesis.[8]

In this longer perspective two earlier precursors of communication through pictorial symbols may be found: Egyptian hieroglyphics and the pictorial battle maps that show size and location of fighting forces. These comparisons also throw some light on the visual qualities – 'style' perhaps – that Isotype developed. The characteristic sobriety and simplicity of the mature Isotype is at once modern and of its time, but yet also relates back to older graphic work: pictorial and semi-pictorial maps, technical drawing and engraving (the plates to the great French *Encyclopédie* are among the best examples here). Neurath collected material of this kind, and it was clearly a source of inspiration for Isotype: occasionally of direct and specific application, and more generally in creating a visual culture within which to work.[9]

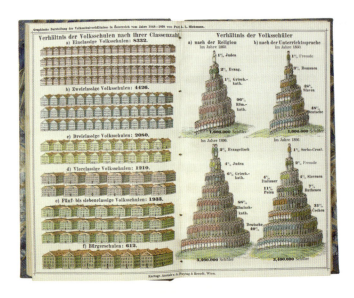

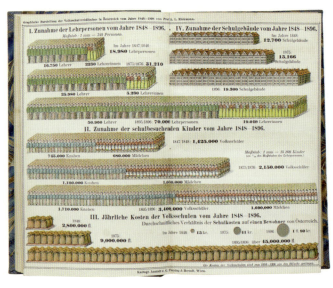

3.02–3.03 Two of the set of charts made by Leo Hickmann for a compendium of information on education in Austria and elsewhere. Despite the appearance of the symbols representing a unit, representation is by length: '1 mm = 340 people' and '1 mm = 14,800 children'. *Zur Geschichte und Statistik des Volksschulwesens im In- und Auslande*, Vienna: Verlag der Sonderausstellungs-Commission 'Jugendhalle', 1898. (198 x 130 mm)

The question of a system

In Isotype there lies the promise of an 'international system of typographic picture education' and, before this name was devised (in
1935), it had become known as the 'Wiener Methode' – the Vienna
method. In its work and in accompanying writings by its makers,
Isotype was put forward as a system or method that may be used to
present material, and particularly quantified information, in pictorial-
diagrammatic form. The suggestion of a set of rules with international applicability is enough to explain our continuing interest in
Isotype.

From its earliest work, Isotype stood by one rule or principle: in
showing quantified information, symbols are used to present a
fixed quantity; greater quantities are shown by the repetition of
symbols [3.04]. This provides a firm basis for the graphic presentation of quantified information, but, by itself, does not provide a
system. Inspection of the large and diverse body of Isotype work
suggests the following: that, from the start (in 1925) it followed its
fundamental rule; that it was informed by other principles, which
emerge, are tested, modified and refined; that these principles were
continually affected by the challenge of new tasks; that the work
was subject to all the mundane pressures of real life, and to the
special traumas of European politics (leading to two forced removals); that it was essentially team-work, with all that this may imply;
that, despite these complicating and perhaps disturbing factors,
Isotype work, from an early date, does have a characteristic and
consistent approach.

In trying to make explicit this (or any other) approach to design
work, there is an inevitable risk of oversimplifying and hardening-
up a complex process. As an interpreter or historian, one is trying
to abstract out the principles that inform the process of turning
information (quantified or otherwise) into visual or graphic form,
so that it makes some intelligible and interesting statement. The
approach cannot be explained or described without detailed study
of particular examples of work; and these would, ideally, need to
be discussed with those responsible for their design. From such a

discussion, reasons and principles behind specific features would become evident, though still perhaps not very easily stated.[10]

One should not make too much of this incommunicability: the Isotype attitude is certainly against any mystification of the design process (as pure and unexplainable creation). But, because it was teamwork and was conducted verbally or through no more than informal sketches and layouts, considerable subtleties could be developed. For example, special adjustments could be made for a particular task – fine adjustments of space to fit a predetermined format, or variations in a normal configuration to suggest a special meaning – and such things are simply not open to formulation in general terms. In spite of these difficulties, it is certainly possible to suggest larger informing principles of Isotype. The explanation of the Isotype design (transformation) process has suggested one such principle: that the point of the work is to make something intelligible and interesting – a positive statement that will reward study.

There is clearly no intention of devising a set of rules by which given material can automatically be translated into visual form. This is the notion of (to paraphrase Otto Neurath) 'turning boring rows of numbers into boring rows of symbols'. Rather, the material is open to questioning: should a selection be made (knowing that a 'visual statement' is soon lost if too much is shown)? The 'interest' that is an aim of Isotype may best be found through comparison of material: a juxtaposition of two or more parts of a whole, or of sets of possibly related material, may provide the necessary stimulus to questioning and thought in a viewer or reader. So Isotype avoids the simple chart that shows only one variable. This attempt to make a visual statement may seem to lead in the direction of a rather free treatment of material. This would be misleading. An equally insistent matter of principle is the need to be faithful to the material and to the viewer. This is a larger reason behind the repetition of symbols. Alternative methods, of enlarging signs or symbols, break this faith:

10. That even the systematized work of Isotype depends considerably on tacit skills was suggested by Michael Macdonald-Ross, in articles that broke with the reductive tendencies within educational psychology: 'Graphics in text', in: L.S. Shulman (ed.), *Review of Research in Education*, vol. 5, 1977; 'How numbers are shown', *Audio-Visual Communication Review*, vol. 25, 1977, pp. 359–409.

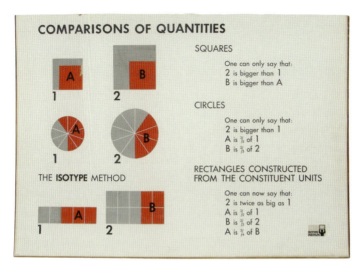

3.04 A variant of the explanation of Isotype principles, here without the further step of using pictorial symbols. This exhibition chart was made around 1933 for showing at the London 'branch' of the GeWiMu; it would have been taken over by the Isotype Institute, and is now in the collection at Reading. (630 x 840 mm)

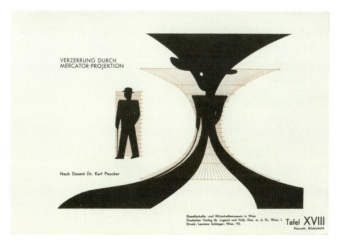

3.05 Demonstration of the distortions embodied in the Mercator projection, based on the work of Karl Peucker, the GeWiMu's consultant cartographer. This is one of a set of charts provided with Otto Neurath's *Bildstatistik nach Wiener Methode in der Schule* (Vienna/Leipzig: Deutscher Verlag für Jugend und Volk, 1933). (150 x 225 mm)

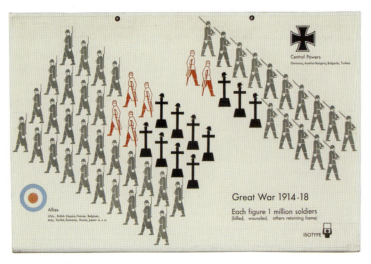

3.06 As with 3.04, this was a chart made around 1933 for showing in London and is now at Reading. The two punched hanging holes at the top suggest that it was used in travelling, short-term displays. (420 x 630 mm)

what is signified by the sign or symbol cannot be read directly, and there may be some suggestion of distortion of material. And in the same spirit, Isotype preferred an equal-area projection for geographical charts against those projections (such as Mercator's) that distort area. [3.05] Parallel rather than perspective projections were used in three-dimensional images. And then this larger principle of fidelity (and a particular kind of matter-of-factness or down-to-earthness) can be seen to inform all the reasoning behind details of design: the use and choice of colours, drawing of symbols, grouping of material, fine decisions in the placing of elements. An Isotype chart on the Great War may serve to illustrate some of these features. [3.06] This was an English-language adaptation of material that had been the basis for successive German-language charts, and it shows something of the sophistication and subtlety of detail that had been achieved by the time it was made (around 1933).

The symbols are placed in a parallel projection, and not on the picture plane in rows or blocks (as would be more usual in Isotype work). As earlier versions of the chart suggest, this would seem to derive from the tradition of battle maps, in which quantified groups of soldiers are shown in a setting that may combine elements of the map and of pictorial landscape. Whatever may be its derivation, the use of this configuration suggests an approach that is prepared to adapt to material, and not a dogmatically applied method. The configuration allows various comparisons to be made: between the sizes of the two opposing whole groups; of proportions within each group; between proportions of the same class across the two groups. Thus the chart can be read in three ways (at least), and this requires some time and attention from the viewer.

The symbols are drawn so that the three classes (of living, wounded, and dead) have approximately equal visual weight, and combine to form a satisfactory whole group; but each class can be easily picked out from the whole group. Living soldiers are grey in colour, wounded are red, the dead are black – and this is further aid to differentiation. On close inspection it may be seen that the symbols of the two groups are distinguished by details of dress and posture; it is in small but significant points like these that one may observe something of the Isotype approach.

Approaches to designing

One can find this way of thinking and working in other examples of design work. As already said, Otto Neurath was proud to situate Isotype in a certain tradition of visual communication. While his stress in those discussions was on specifically pictorial communication, it seems worth considering a larger sense of 'visual communication', to include any kind of presentation that acts out meanings visually (the usual opposition here is to the merely verbal or textual). We can thus include any kind of abstracted or non-figurative representation: the field is enlarged to take in diagrams, text that is given visual form, buildings, gardens, town planning ... This discussion could be extended even further, to cover any kind of ordering process in which configuration takes the content and meanings of the material as its main guide. We could thus consider the planning of a meal, of a musical concert, or a medical investigation. For this occasion, I will confine the illustrations to a first level of extension.

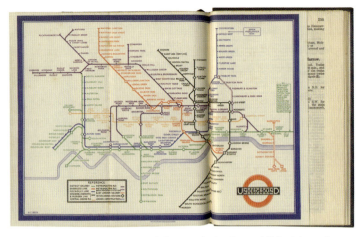

3.07 The London Underground diagram in its first published form, in 1933. This copy was included in the book edited by Findlay Muirhead: *Short guide to London*, 3rd edn, London: Ernest Benn Limited, 1933. (Size of the diagram sheet: 155 x 223 mm)

Beck

The London Underground diagram, now so much celebrated as a design classic, shares something with Isotype.[11] [3.07] One can notice that this was an invention by someone (Harry Beck) who was not a professional designer or graphic artist, and could approach the matter unconventionally and freshly. Beck's first sketch for the diagram was made in 1931 – and is thus coeval with our subject. Commonly referred to as the 'London Underground map', it may better, as its chief historian has insisted, be called a diagram.[12] What is shown are not so much geographical relations, but rather connective relations. One travels under the ground, without any reference to a passing context or landscape, and the most important thing to know are the connections, the interchanges. In a similar way, Isotype throws out

---

11. That something is shared between Isotype and the Underground diagram was noticed also by Richard Hollis in his *Graphic design: a concise history*, London: Thames & Hudson, 1994, p. 18.
12. Ken Garland, *Mr Beck's Underground map*, Harrow Weald: Capital Transport, 1994.

a good deal of detail, making a radical selection of what it is really necessary to know.

In both Beck's diagram and in Isotype, information is conveyed visually. Colour is loaded with meaning and becomes an essential part of the way both work. In both, a highly considered set of forms is used. One sees a strict set of conventions and constraints at work. In the Underground diagram, the angles of the lines are restricted, the distances between stations are placed at regular intervals. Both are designed with a standardizing mentality. Yet both were made by restlessly curious and self-critical designers, who wanted to go on changing and experimenting with what they had done. Both were able to accommodate new expanded and updated information.

Tschichold

Other contemporary instances of like-minded thinking can be found in Jan Tschichold's expositions of the New Typography.[13] In his book *Die neue Typographie* (1928), he expounds the virtues of standardized formats, then recently issued by the DIN. A key example is the standard for letterheadings, which lays down a given size (A4) and given fields for the different elements of the document. Within these limits, the designer is free. The letterheadings reproduced here show the Tschicholdian ideas very clearly. [3.08] In the version preferred by the client (right), the information is set in a block, with lines run on in disregard of their sense. Even the name of the organization has some ambiguity to it in this setting. In Tschichold's design (left), the organization is now clearly stated: Arbeitsgemeinschaft des Bayerischen Kunstgewerbevereins und des Münchner Bundes. Then the members of its directing committee are clearly stated, strung out in a list. The second colour (red) is put to work more effectively in the redesign, to point and underscore the information. Note the way in which red is reserved for the parts originating with the issuing organization ('Unser Zeichen' [our reference], 'Tag' [date]), 'Betreff' [the subject], while black is kept for the information from the addressee: 'Ihre Zeichen' [your reference], 'Ihre Nachricht vom' [your letter of ...]). This is a

13. Tschichold was drawn to Vienna to work briefly at the Gesellschafts- und Wirtschaftsmuseum. See Christopher Burke, *Active literature*, Hyphen Press, 2007, pp. 119–21.

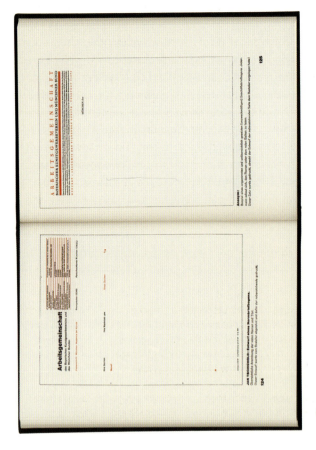

kunstmuseum luzern | 24. februar bis 31. märz 1935

**these
antithese
synthese**

arp
braque
calder
chirico
derain
erni
ernst
fernandez
giacometti
gonzalez
gris
helion
kandinsky
klee
leger
miro
mondrian
nicholson
paalen
ozenfant
picasso
tauber-arp

meaning-determined attitude to graphic devices that shares much with the attitude of Isotype.

The device of the list, in which all the constituent components are strung out one after the other, in a proud display, became a characteristic device of Tschichold's New Typography. [3.09] In this list of artists, however, alphabetical order is used. Alphabetical is a good way to deal with a number of ego-conscious subjects, but in Isotype one would search for a more inherent principle of order.

Bill

This kind of thinking can inform all areas of design, and of course Isotype charts were made as part of a larger effort of design – the making of exhibitions and museums. It must be worth suggesting how this approach can occur in designing buildings. An example is the Hochschule für Gestaltung at Ulm, designed by Max Bill in the late 1940s, early 1950s. [3.10] (This drawing, incidentally, is an equal-dimensioned, axonometric that shares something with Isotype practice.) The HfG Ulm is a case of a 'legible building', whose functions are clearly grouped and separated. The classrooms are at the left in this drawing; then the common, social parts in the central blocks; and then to the right, living accommodation. In fact only three of the residential blocks were built (a low 'atelier' unit, a tower, another atelier unit). But in the full scheme shown here one sees the idea of the line of units extending until it stops. As in Isotype, one finds the idea of the units being repeated, strung out. Further: the whole building hugs the terrain, reflecting its rise and fall (the low teaching

[facing page]
3.08 Two letterheadings included in Jan Tschichold, *Die neue Typographie* (Berlin: Bildungsverband der deutschen Buchdrucker, 1928; this reproduction is from the facsimile edition, published in 1987). Tschichold's caption on the left-hand page reads: 'The client rejected this design and the one shown opposite was printed in its place.' And on the right page: 'This setting was printed, despite the one opposite having been presented to the client!' (210 x 148 mm)
3.09 Catalogue cover designed by Jan Tschichold, 1935, reproduced from his *Leben und Werk des Typographen Jan Tschichold*, Dresden: VEB, 1977. (205 x 142 mm)

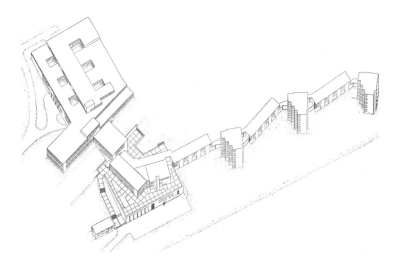

3.10 Drawing of the Hochschule für Gestaltung Ulm, reproduced from *HFG Ulm: Programm wird Bau*, Stuttgart: Edition Solitude, 1998.

parts are higher; the living quarters are on lower ground). The design takes account of and is partly shaped by its material. At the centre of the ensemble is the bar, whose curved form breaks with the rectangular forms of the rest of the building. Here a difference of form speaks out the meaning: this is the sociable heart of the building.

Froshaug
In this postcard-sized display, dating from 1951, the printer and designer Anthony Froshaug listed the types that he owned and which he could offer to his customers in the printing he was doing for them. It shows a number of features that bear similarities with the Isotype approach.[14] [3.11]

The material is configured in vertical alignments that recall, for example, the 'Beschäftigten in den Gewerbebetrieben des Deutschen Reiches' charts. [2.13–2.15] One sees here too a central column of

14. As he told me, Anthony Froshaug was an admirer of Isotype. His first published piece of writing was a review of the film *World of plenty*, mentioning the Isotype diagrams in it ('World of plenty' in: *Anthony Froshaug: Typography & texts*, Hyphen Press, 2000, pp. 90–2).

fixed width (the samples of the typefaces), with rows that extend to the left (point sizes) and right (names, dates, and makers). In the left column, positioning of the elements is determined by their place in the sequence of type sizes. So if there is no type of a certain size in stock, then the place is empty. Black numbers mean that the printer already has the type in that size; red numbers mean that he intends to buy that size. So, colour is used for meaning, and the disposition of the red numbers and names speaks out a story that is unfolding. This is one of a series of these cards that Froshaug made; each 'edition' was an updated report on his stocks of type.

Notice how the types are grouped: first by category (modern, egyptian, eccentric, sans serif), and then by date of design or first manufacture. So here too, as with Isotype, the ordering of the material is given consideration – is determined by meaning – and then the ordering determines the disposition of the material: the 'design' of it. The simplest, also least intelligent course of action here would have been to order the types alphabetically.

Finally, one can notice that the showing of the images of each type – actual examples are printed – constitutes a kind of pictorial approach: a move in the direction of a type specimen, rather than just a type list.

		anthony froshaug msia		cucurrian	ludgvan	pz	cwll	
Moderns			18 14	10 8		äAal⅛	Monotype Bodoni 135 . [c1786 . Bodoni]
		24	18	12 10 8		Aal	Monotype Bodoni Italic 135 I
		24		14 12 10 8		A*l* 1	Monotype Bodoni Heavy 260
		24	18	12 8		Aa	Minster Black . 1815 . Figgins
	36		18	12		I	Fat Face . 1820–1842 . Thorowgood
	36		18	12		AAa	Thorowgood Italic . 1820 . Thorowgood
				12		Aal	Fat Face Contra Italic . 1834 . Thorowgood
		28				A	Argentine . c1860 . Besley
Eccentrics Egyptians			18	12		Aal	Egyptian . 182– . Austin [?]
	36		24	12		Aal	Egyptian Expanded . Figgins . 1847
			22			A1	Union Pearl . c1674–90 . Grover [?]
		28					Rustic Shaded . 1845 . Figgins
				12		Aal	Freehand Script . 1895 . Stephenson , Blake
		24	14			Aal	Marina Script . 1937 . Stephenson , Blake
Sans Serifs	36		24	18	10 8 6	äAal⅛	Monotype Gill Sans 262 . 1927 . Gill
	36		24		14 12 10 8 6	äAal	Monotype Gill Sans Italic 262 I . 1929 . Gill
	36		24	18 14 12	8 6	Aal	Monotype Gill Bold 275 . 1929 . Gill

3.11 Type list designed and printed by Anthony Froshaug, 1951. Designed as a postcard, this was included within Froshaug's second 'conspectus' of his printing, from which it is reproduced here. (105 x 148 mm)

 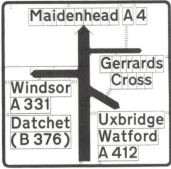

3.12–3.13 A United Kingdom road sign that follows the system devised by Jock Kinneir and Margaret Calvert. The principles for making these signs were demonstrated in the diagram shown here. (Photograph made in 2001, near Natland, Cumbria)

Kinneir / Calvert

Isotype is often mentioned in connection with the symbols used on road signs, and in connection with the whole field of symbols and signs in the environment. A more subtle, perhaps deeper Isotype character can be seen in the system by which the United Kingdom road signs were made, following the set of principles devised in the early 1960s by the designer Jock Kinneir and his assistant Margaret Calvert.

These road signs are made by local authorities, and a chief problem for Kinneir and Calvert was to lay down a set of quite high-level guidelines that could yet be understood and put to use by council officers, who were not professional designers. This may be the situation of any design effort that wants its work to achieve widespread and consistent application; Isotype can be included here. If the UK road signs are now in a state of over-abundant and uncoordinated disarray, forty years after the reform, this is hardly the fault of Kinneir and Calvert – rather it is a consequence of unceasing too-little-considered change in central government's policy for roads and the signs that are placed by them. The sign shown here [3.12] is evidence of the system as it was intended.

The secret of the system lies in a diagram that gives the rules of lay-out. [3.13] A unit, which is the width of the stem of one of the characters, is used to position the names, and to find the thickness of directional lines and other elements. The whole ensemble is then as big as it needs to be: it has no set dimensions. Of course there are still variables. Someone has to decide what should be said on the sign. There were rules for that too, but still there was scope for interpretation.

After Isotype

We can learn much from Isotype, but we cannot simply and unproblematically continue it. Even if it was possible to distil some method or system out of this work, the conditions in which we now live and work are too different from those in which it was made and put to use.

There have been some attempts to engage more intelligently with the Isotype legacy than by simple-minded continuation. Cases that I know about are the work done in the 1970s at the Institute of Educational Technology in the Open University (UK), and at the Natural History Museum in London, where the idea of the transformer was taken up and used in the small groups that were working in these institutions to make publications, teaching materials, exhibition displays. For a time in the late 1970s, the IET issued a series of 'Notes on transforming'. 'What is a transformer?', 'Three functions of text presentation', 'Numbering systems in text' were among the titles of these informal publications.[15]

15. While the publications of the IET may be hard to find now, at least one article was published in a more accessible publication: Michael Macdonald-Ross and Robert Waller, 'The transformer', *Penrose Annual*, vol. 69, pp. 141–52; republished with additions as 'The transformer revisited', *Information Design Journal*, vol. 9, nos. 2–3, 2000, pp. 177–93. R.S. Miles wrote about 'transformation' in a book he co-edited: *The design of educational exhibitions*, London: George Allen & Unwin, 1982. See also his 'Otto Neurath and the modern public museum: the case of the Natural History Museum (London)', in Nemeth & Stadler, *Encyclopedia and utopia*, pp. 183–90.

At both the IET and the Natural History Museum inspiration from Isotype could be found in the idea of a small group of people of different specialisms working together on a project, with the work being held together by a central co-ordinating figure, responsible to the rest of the group and representing also the interests of those who will use the material produced. This is the transformer, seen by the Otto and Marie Neurath as 'the trustee of the public'. The museum was the place where these ideas were developed, and it is a natural place for their continued use.

If the examples of work by others that I have presented here can be related to the Isotype way of thinking, then it becomes clear that Isotype takes its place in the large and fruitful field of 'design for meaning'. In this way of working, one tries as a designer (in the widest sense of that word) to make sense of the material and let it find good order, both for the sake of the material itself and for the sake of the people reading and using it. The two dimensions – the material and its users – become indivisible. It can come as a relief to see the work of Otto Neurath and his colleagues in this way. One can then forget about schemes for writing programs to generate Isotype charts automatically, or attempts to update the Isotype symbols for the multicultural societies of the twenty-first century, or any other such hopeful idea that this work can be divorced from the people who made it, from the technics with which they worked, and from the social and cultural contexts in which they worked. Their work is rich with suggestions that can be picked up, digested, transferred, extrapolated from – not just in making graphic presentations of quantitative data, but in designing material of any kind.

4

Marie Neurath, 1898 – 1986

Marie Neurath died in London on 10 October 1986.[1] Her work with Otto Neurath on what became known as Isotype is now well documented, not least by her own spare and lucid writings. The remarks that follow will not attempt a systematic description of her life and work, but are meant as an informal and personal statement.

In some of the autobiographical texts that she wrote, Marie Neurath fixed on the first moments of an experience or a relationship, as assuming special significance. The first occasion that I can remember is of her moving around a studio at the Typography Unit (as it then was) at the University of Reading. After she had given the materials of the 'Otto and Marie Neurath Isotype Collection' to the University, she came regularly to hold a seminar about Isotype with third-year students of typography. I was then only in the second year: that I could not go to the seminar (and that an 'ad hoc' student from the Netherlands sitting next to me could) was a source of considerable frustration and jealousy.

Marie's qualities were visible already from across the room: her uprightness, both in posture and, as one discovered, in the moral sense too; her natural dignity, and lack of pretension and ceremony; her sense of equality and her openness, so that there were never any barriers from difference of age. I wanted to get to know her. The first chance came in 1975, when we made an exhibition on Isotype at Reading. Then I wrote an MPhil thesis on the subject, and our contact continued with the cataloguing of the Collection. In the last years it was centred on the translation of and editorial work on Otto Neurath's writings, which was her major preoccupation after closing the Isotype Institute office.

Marie Neurath (née Reidemeister) came from Braunschweig in North Germany. The decisive moment in her life came in September 1924, when, on a student trip to Vienna, she was introduced to Otto Neurath and decided – instinctively – that she wanted to work with him. There followed what one may see as her central years (1925 – 34), immersed in this work and in the life of the new Vienna of democratic-socialist reform.

---

1. This obituary was first published in *Information Design Journal*, vol. 5, no. 1, 1986, pp. 69 – 71, and reprinted in my book *Unjustified texts* (Hyphen Press, 2002). It is given here without much change, despite some duplication of content elsewhere in the present work.

In her accounts of the history of Isotype, Marie tended to play down her own part – as we gradually came to realize at Reading. Though latterly she did hint that Otto Neurath would never have embarked on the project of a 'Gesellschafts- und Wirtschaftsmuseum in Wien' without her. The history of their work, as it developed subsequently, supports this suggestion. When the Isotype Institute was set up in England in 1942, Otto and Marie were directors on equal terms. And, after Otto's death in 1945, Marie continued its work for nearly thirty years, concentrating on the production of educational books for young readers. The achievement of these books, seen in the context of their time, has yet to be properly assessed.

Otto Neurath was an encyclopaedist in the Enlightenment tradition, with multiple and academically unorthodox interests, of which Isotype was perhaps the strangest – especially to his associates who were respectably employed in universities, as Neurath was not. For Marie, this visual work was the leading activity of her life, and it perfectly suited her. She had wide cultural and social interests, and trained to be a teacher, specializing in mathematics and physics. She also had a strongly visual side to her and had done a course in drawing at art school.

The character of Isotype – if one can personify it – followed from the interests and dispositions of the people behind it, Otto and Marie above all. It was concerned with the visual representation of things that needed to be said: not just any facts, but information worth presenting, and from which one could learn historical and social relationships, as well as facts. Isotype was not, as in the popular image of it, a simple method for turning numbers into pictorial statistics. Rather, and at its best, Isotype charts were intelligent visual statements, which were developed freshly on each occasion from a set of partly tacit principles. I once tried to say some of this in an essay about the possible uses of Isotype.[2] What I did not say there was that, despite Otto Neurath's wish for a widely diffused and perhaps international 'picture language', to think of an Isotype that was not a product of the collaboration of – most essentially – Otto Neurath, Marie Neurath, Gerd Arntz, is to imagine something different and probably something reduced in quality. The history of attempts by others to make 'isotypes' (as they are sometimes misleadingly called) shows this.

In Isotype terminology, Marie was the 'transformer': the person who made the visual statements, and the crucial intermediary between those with specialist knowledge, those who assembled the final product, and – in some respects the most important element – the public. Otto and Marie never used the term 'designer' (in English or in German equivalents). But

2. 'On the influence of Isotype', *Information Design Journal*, vol. 2, no. 2, 1981, pp. 122–30.

4.01 Marie Neurath, summer 1984.
(Photograph by Gertrud Neurath)

this word has only in recent years resumed its special sense of someone who plans and gives material form to content; and when, at Reading, we used to speak of the transformer as a designer, Marie would be doubtful. She assumed that designers were visual decorators who changed the form of things every season, following fashion. (There are, alas, considerable grounds for this belief.) In contrast and as its name indicates, Isotype was standards-minded: if you have arrived, after considerable invention and experiment, at a satisfactory symbol or configuration of symbols, why change it? Marie stood for continuities, in spite of the tragedies of the times that she lived through. A story from her life illustrates this attitude. With Otto, she had left The Hague at the last moment in May 1940, in a small open boat. After the war, she returned to The Hague on a visit, and there used up the tram tickets that remained from a pre-war packet. They had travelled with her through the escape, some months in internment, and then an intensely busy and happy period (up to Otto Neurath's death in December 1945) in Oxford, where the Isotype Institute was first established.

Her life was extraordinarily productive. The Isotype Collection at Reading includes many boxes of working materials, and I suppose that similar small mountains of stuff got lost in the two forced removals, from Vienna and from The Hague. She had a beautiful economy of effort. In correcting translations, she would suggest the minimum necessary changes, often finding one or two words which then solved what had seemed an impossibly complicated problem. In this translation and editorial work, her passion for accuracy was vivid to those of us who knew her only in the last phase of her life: looking at the products of Isotype, one can see this same quality informing them. And as well as her concern for accurate and honest statement, she had a phenomenally exact memory: she was an exemplary recorder of events.

The later years were enriched by new friendships with people who came to see her about Otto, but quickly became devoted to Marie. One by one, we came under her spell, and now form a still growing group of Neurath specialists in at least five countries. She was the very opposite of the tiresome widow who stifles free discussion of her husband's work. Though certainly a partisan of Otto Neurath's work, Marie applied no pressures. Our interest in Otto Neurath became a matter of common exploration with her. Another story: someone had published a selection of Otto Neurath's writings, prefaced by a long interpretative introduction, which he wrote without consulting her. She compiled a long list of points of query or disagreement. He came to discuss these. I asked her how the meeting had gone. She said, rather surprised, 'well, he agreed with me on every point'. They were soon on 'du' terms, and then he would come regularly to London, just because he loved her.

Her main regret, in her last days, was that further progress had not been made on the various editions of Otto Neurath's writings that are in progress. These include a selection (in English) of his writings on economics, which was especially important for her. There is also an edition of the correspondence with Rudolf Carnap (in English and also in German), and the collected writings on visual education (in German). A short, well-illustrated book on Isotype is also planned, and the last text she wrote was for this. These books will appear eventually, and they will further confirm the significance of the life and work of Otto Neurath.[3] This process of the discovery of Otto Neurath (he was never well enough known for it to be called a rediscovery) has been and will be one of Marie's great achievements. Those of us involved in these books will miss her especially. And, writing this now, it is hard to realize that I can no longer telephone her to arrange a visit for us to go through this text, drink coffee, and get on to talk about books, politics, people.

[1986]

3. Of the books mentioned in this paragraph, only one of them has been published: Otto Neurath's *Gesammelte bildpädagogische Schriften*.

Sources

The literature of and about Otto Neurath's visual work is now extensive, dispersed, and growing. This guide points to the principal sources, with no claims to completeness.

Some web pages compiled by Co Seegers on Otto Neurath and 'pictorial statistics' may provide the best listings on the subject at the time of writing (January 2009): http://members.chello.nl/j.seegers1/ottoneurath/neurath.html.

There are useful bibliographies of writings by the Neuraths, and of books and articles with Isotype contributions, in the catalogue of an exhibition: *Graphic communication through Isotype* (Reading: Department of Typography & Graphic Communication, University of Reading, 1975, 2nd edn. 1981). From this phase of research came another book associated with an exhibition, edited by Friedrich Stadler: *Arbeiterbildung in der Zwischenkriegszeit: Otto Neurath – Gerd Arntz* (Vienna: Löcker Verlag, 1982).

The Otto & Marie Neurath Isotype Collection, at the Department of Typography & Graphic Communication, University of Reading, is the main archive of this work. 'Isotype revisited' is a research project at this Department, due to finish in 2010, which promises to provide a thorough documentation of all aspects of the subject. Meanwhile, my own MPhil thesis ('Otto Neurath's contribution to visual communication 1925 – 1945: the history, graphic language and theory of Isotype', University of Reading, 1979) is still useful for a detailed analysis of the visual conventions of the work.

Apart from archival sources and the publications that were made by the Neurath group, the best sources are writings by the principal participants: Otto Neurath and Marie Neurath. Otto Neurath's writings on visual matters have been collected as the *Gesammelte bildpädagogische Schriften* (Vienna: Hölder-Pichler-Tempsky, 1991), edited by Rudolf Haller and myself. This was published as one volume in a projected collection of all of Neurath's writings. In Neurath's lifetime he published many short pieces and two more extended considerations: *Bildstatistik nach Wiener Methode in der Schule* (Vienna/Leipzig: Deutscher Verlag für Jugend und Volk, 1933) and *International picture language* (London: Kegan Paul, 1936). *International picture language* was reprinted, with a German translation added, by the Department of Typography & Graphic Communication, University of Reading, in 1980.

Among several books about Neurath's work as a whole, one can men-

121

tion: Elisabeth M. Nemeth and Friedrich Stadler (ed.), *Encyclopedia and utopia: the life and work of Otto Neurath, 1882–1945* (Dordrecht/Boston: Kluwer, 1996), and Nancy Cartwright (with others), *Otto Neurath: philosophy between science and politics* (Cambridge: Cambridge University Press, 1995).

During the time of the work, up to about 1960, Marie Neurath published occasional articles on its methods. In her later years, and especially after her retirement in 1971, she wrote and edited contributions that were more historical in nature. Two more extended pieces are: 'Otto Neurath and Isotype', *Graphic Design* [Japan], no. 42, 1971, pp. 11–30; 'Isotype', *Instructional Science*, vol. 3, no. 2, 1974, pp. 127–50. She also edited with Robert Cohen an anthology of writings by and about Otto Neurath: *Empiricism and sociology* (Dordrecht: Reidel, 1973).

Gerd Arntz's work has been documented in a number of Dutch publications, especially the catalogue of a retrospective exhibition, *Gerd Arntz: kritische grafiek en beeldstatistiek* (The Hague: Haagse Gemeentemusem, 1976) and his own book, edited by Kees Broos, *De tijd onder het mes: hout- & linoleumsneden 1920–1970* (Nijmegen: SUN, 1988).

After the documentation that was done in the 1970s and early 1980s, there seemed to be a pause in interest. This pause has now come to an end, with a number of publications and exhibitions. These include: the book by Frank Hartmann and Erwin K. Bauer, *Bildersprache: Otto Neurath / Visualisierung* (Vienna: WUV Universitätsverlag, 2002); an exhibition shown in Brno, Prague, Vienna, and finally at the Triennale in Milan (2002–3); a book by Nader Vossoughian, *Otto Neurath: the language of the global polis* (Rotterdam: NAI Publishers, 2008), with an associated exhibition and events at the Stroom gallery in The Hague; a website of Gerd Arntz's graphic work (www.gerdarntz.org), and a book by Ed Annink and Max Bruinsma, *Lovely language* (Rotterdam: Veenman, 2008). For some discussion of these works, see my website post: http://www.hyphenpress.co.uk/journal/2008/05/12/isotype_recent_publications.

Hadwig Kraeutler's *Otto Neurath, museum and exhibition work: spaces (designed) for communication* (Frankfurt: Peter Lang, 2008)–a development of the author's PhD thesis–breaks fresh ground in its consideration of this aspect of Neurath's work.

Index

Marie Neurath and Otto Neurath have not been indexed, nor has 'transformation' and 'transformer': they are present on most pages. The main topic of this book is indexed under 'Isotype, principles'. '40c' refers to a caption on page 40, '111n' refers to a note on page 111.

Active literature (Burke), 111n
A few ounces a day (Rotha) 61
Peter Alma (1886–1969) 44
Ed Annink 122
Arbeit, Wohlstand und das Glück der Menschheit (Wells) 38c
Arbeiterbildung in der Zwischenkriegszeit (Stadler) 121
Gerd Arntz (1900–88) 22, 27, 47, 59, 60c, 84, 87, 122
Gerd Arntz: kritische grafiek en beeldstatistiek 122
Atlas (Berghaus) 55
www.gerdarntz.org 122
Obafemi Awolowo (1909–87) 72

Baines Dixon Collection 8
Basic English 13c, 46, 47–9
Basic by Isotype (Otto Neurath) 46, 47–9
Erwin K. Bauer 122
Friedrich Bauermeister 28
Harry Beck (1903–74) 108–9
Mr Beck's Underground map (Garland) 108n
James R. Beniger 96n
Berghaus 55
Erwin Bernath (1901–79) 16
Bibliographisches Institut, Leipzig 27
Bildersprache (Hartmann & Bauer) 122
Bildstatistik nach Wiener Methode in der Schule (Otto Neurath) 45, 105c, 121
Max Bill (1908–94) 111–12
Robert Bleichsteiner (1891–1954) 28, 29
'Blind eyes, innuendo and the politics of design' (Kinross) 100n
Willard C. Brinton (1880–1957) 99–100
Kees Broos 122
Max Bruinsma 122

Die bunte Welt 8, 14, 16c, 19c, 20, 20c, 27–8, 27c–28c, 30, 35, 84c, 91c, 93c
Christopher Burke 7, 109n
De Bijenkorf 56c, 57–8, 59c

Cable & Wireless 68
Margaret Calvert (1936–) 115
Rudolf Carnap (1891–1970) 120
Nancy Cartwright 121
Gordon Childe (1892–1957) 63, 65
Clive Chizlett 99n
Robert Cohen 122
The commercial and political atlas (Playfair) 99
Common Ground 68
Compton's Pictured Encyclopedia 52c, 53c, 54–5
Patricia Costigan-Eaves 96n

'Damned lies and statistics' (Chizlett) 100n
'Data graphics in the 20th century' (Costigan-Eaves) 96n
The design of educational exhibitions (Miles & others) 115n
Deutsches Hygienemuseum, Dresden 51
Dictionary of statistics (Mulhall) 98, 98c

Early thematic mapping in the history of cartography 100n
Education for all in the Western Region 72c–74c
Empiricism and sociology (Otto Neurath) 8, 100n, 122
Encyclopedia and utopia (Nemeth & Stadler) 122
Encyclopédie (Diderot & d'Alembert) 101

123

Die Entwicklung von Landwirtschaft und Gewerbe in Deutschland 18, 94

Alois Fischer (1897–?) 28, 29
Mary Fleddérus 45
Wolfgang Foges (1910–83) 63, 65, 72
Josef Frank (1885–1967) 23
From cave painting to comic strip (Hogben) 100n
'From hieroglyphics to Isotype' (Otto Neurath) 96n, 97
Anthony Froshaug (1920–84) 112–13
Anthony Froshaug: Typography & texts (Kinross) 112n
H. Gray Funkhouser (1898–1984) 96n

Ken Garland (1929–) 108n
Gesammelte bildpädagogische Schriften (Otto Neurath) 8, 96n, 120n, 121
Gesellschaft und Wirtschaft 8, 27, 28–44, 45, 46, 54, 90n
Gesellschafts- und Wirtschaftsmuseum in Wien 8, 11, 13, 16–18, 22–6, 28, 45–6, 77, 78, 84, 87, 109n, 118, and see: Isotype, locations
'Gesolei', 18
Die Gewerkschaften 18
Graphic communication through Isotype (University of Reading) 121
Graphic design: a concise history (Hollis) 108n
Graphic methods for presenting facts (Brinton) 99–100
Graphic presentation (Brinton) 100n
'Graphics in text' (Macdonald-Ross) 104n

Rudolf Haller (1929–) 121
Frank Hartmann 122
Heinemann, publisher 71
Leo Hickmann (1834–1906) 102c
'Historical development of the graphical representation of statistical data' (Funkhouser) 96n
Emil Hitschmann 18c
Hochschule für Gestaltung Ulm (HfG) 111–12
HfG Ulm: Programm wird Bau 112c
Lancelot Hogben (1895–1975) 100n

Richard Hollis (1934–) 108n
'How numbers are shown' (Macdonald-Ross) 104n

Gustav Ichheiser (1897–1969) 58
Institute of Educational Technology in the Open University, UK 115, 116
International Encyclopedia of Unified Science 55
International Foundation for Visual Education 47c
International picture language (Neurath) 8, 13c, 14, 46, 47, 48–9, 65, 100n, 121
ISOTYPE
name 47
locations
Amsterdam 45
Berlin-Kreuzberg 45, 84
Bilston 75
The Hague 47–61, 119
London 45, 66–71, 105c, 106c, 118
Mexico City 53
Moscow 45
New York 45, 51
Oxford 61–5, 66, 118, 119
Vienna 8, 11–13, 16–46, 78–9, 117, 118
Western Nigeria 72–5
media
books 18, 27–28, 46, 47–9, 54–5, 58–61, 62–5, 66, 68, 71, 72–3
exhibitions 16–18, 23–6, 51, 57–8
film 26, 61–2
filmstrips 68, 70, 71, 75
principles
axial configuration 13, 19–20, 31, 34c, 36, 37c, 80, 91, 94
bars not graphs 13c
colour 20, 22–3, 29c, 31c, 32c, 33c, 34c, 35c, 38c, 39c, 41c, 51, 52c, 56c, 58, 69c, 107, 109, 113
comparison 99c, 107
consistency 22, 34c, 35c, 41c, 43c, 44
content (not magnitude) determines arrangement 35, 36c, 80, 98, 107, 110, 112, 113, 114–15
countability 13, 20, 26, 36c, 37c, 85, 87

density 11, 36, 53c
equal area representation 30, 106
'Führungsbilder' 20, 27n, 91, 94
geographical order 35, 36c
interesting content 103, 104, 118
maps 23, 25, 28, 30–1, 35, 44
multiple levels of meaning 26, 107
neutrality 26, 106
non-perspective 66, 106
'not more than one knows' 79
parts of a whole (and percentages)
19–20, 36, 88–91, 93, 95
pictorial 113
reading direction 14, 81, 82, 87
repetition (not enlargement) 79, 84,
98, 99–100, 103, 104, 110, 111–12
standardization 43c, 109
symbol design 13, 14, 21–2, 44, 48,
84, 85, 86, 89–91, 107
tabular configuration 54c, 64c, 112
'Isotype' (Marie Neurath) 122
Isotype Institute, Oxford then London
65, 75, 118, 119
'Isotype revisited', 8, 9, 123

Friedrich Jahnel 18

Heinz Kaufler (1913–42) 45
Frits Kerdijk (1879–1972) 51
Eric Kindel 7, 8
Jock Kinneir (1917–94) 114
Robin Kinross (1949–) 8, 76, 99n, 117,
120, 121, 122
Mary van Kleeck (1883–1972) 45
Harry E. Kleinschmidt 51
Alfred A. Knopf (1892–1984) 58
Herbert Koberstein 99n
Kosmos (Humboldt) 55
Hadwig Kraeutler 122

Joseph Lauwerys (1902–81) 62, 65
Leben und Werk des Typographen Jan
Tschichold 111n
Professor Lehmann 25, 28
Living in early times 63c, 64c
Leonora Wilhelmina Lockhart (1906–?)
49
Lovely language (Annink & Bruinsma)
122

Michael Macdonald-Ross 104n, 115n
Machines which work for man 69c
E.J. Marey (1830–1904) 96n
Professor Mendizabal 53
Mercator [Gerard de Kremer] (1512–94)
105c, 106
Meyers Konversationslexikon 46
R.S. Miles 115n
Ministry of Health, The Netherlands 57
Ministry of Health, Western Nigeria 73
Ministry of Information, UK 62
Modern man in the making (Otto
Neurath) 8, 20, 21c, 35, 59–61
Findlay Muirhead 108c
Henk Mulder (1921–98) 10n
Michael G. Mulhall (1836–1900) 98,
99c
Franz Carl Müller-Lyer (1857–1916)
22c, 23
Museum of War Economy, Leipzig 101

National Tuberculosis Association, New
York 50c, 51–2
Natural History Museum, London 115,
116
Elisabeth M. Nemeth (1951–) 122
Die neue Typographie (Tschichold) 109–
11
Marie Neurath [née Reidemeister]
(1898–1986) throughout
Olga Neurath [née Hahn] (1882–1937)
11
Otto Neurath (1882–1945) throughout
Otto and Marie Neurath Isotype
Collection, University of Reading 7,
8, 100n, 105c, 106c, 117, 119, 121
'Otto Neurath and Isotype' (Marie
Neurath) 122
Otto Neurath: the language of the global
polis (Vossoughian) 100n, 122
'Otto Neurath and the modern public
museum' (Miles) 115n
Otto Neurath, museum and exhibition
work (Kraeutler) 122
Otto Neurath: philosophy between
science and politics (Cartwright) 122
'Otto Neurath's contribution to
visual communication 1925–1945'
(Kinross) 117, 121

'Notes on transforming' (IET, Open
   University) 115

C.K. Ogden (1889–1957) 46, 48, 49
'On the influence of Isotype' (Kinross)
   96n
Österreichische Gemeinde-Zeitung 8,
   12c, 15c, 17c, 18c, 78n, 79c, 81c, 82c,
   83c
Österreichischer Verband für
   Siedlungs- und Kleingartenwesen 16

Max Parrish 65, 66, 68, 71
Karl Peucker (1859–1940) 28, 29–31,
   105c
William Playfair (1759–1823) 96n,
   97–8

'Quantitative graphics in statistics'
   (Beniger & Robyn) 96n
François Quesnay (1694–1774) 45, 46c

Railways under London 66–7
Kurt Reidemeister (1893–1971) 11
Rembrandt van Rijn (1606–1669) 57–8
'Het Rollende Rad' 58, 59c
'Rondom Rembrandt' 56c, 57–8
Arthur H. Robinson (1915–2004) 100
Dorothy L. Robyn 96n
Paul Rotha [Paul Thompson] (1907–84)
   61–2, 65
Josef Scheer 16
Wolfgang Schumann 100n
Dr Schwieger 28, 31
Co Seegers (1950–) 121
Short guide to London (Muirhead) 108c
Siedlungsmuseum, Vienna 10n, 11, 100
John Snow (1813–58) 96n
Friedrich Stadler (1951–) 121, 122
Städtische Versicherungsanstalt,
   Vienna 58
The statistical breviary (Playfair) 97
Statistik in Bildern (Koberstein) 99n
Josef Strygowski (1862–1941) 28

These, Antithese, Synthese 110, 111c
*They lived like this in ancient
   Mesopotamia* (Marie Neurath &
   Worboys) 70c–71c

Hans Thomas (1903–?) 44
'The transformer' (Macdonald-Ross &
   Waller) 115n
'The transformer revisited' (Macdonald-
   Ross & Waller) 115n
Trio, printers 51
Jan Tschichold (1902–74) 109–11
August Tschinkel (1905–83) 44
*Tuberculosis: basic facts in picture
   language* 50
Edward Tufte (1942–) 96n
Michael Twyman (1934–) 7, 75
De tijd onder het mes (Arntz) 122

University of Göttingen 11
University of Reading 7, 76, 78,
   100n, 105c, 106c, 117, 121, and see:
   'Otto and Marie Neurath Isotype
   Collection'

Vereinigung Österreichischer
   Betriebsorganisatoren 18c
'Visual autobiography' (Otto Neurath)
   96n, 97, 100n, 101
*The visual display of quantitative
   information* (Tufte) 96n
Visual explanations (Tufte) 96n
'Visual history of mankind', 64–7, 70
'Visual science', 70
Nader Vossoughian 99n, 122

Robert Waller 115n
'Wien und die Wiener' 17
'Wiener Methode' 41
'"Wiener Methode der Bildstatistik"
   und "International System of
   Typographic Picture Education"
   (Isotype)' (Koberstein) 99n
Rotimi Williams (1920–2005) 75
World of plenty (Rotha) 112n
World Social Economic Congress (1931)
   45, 46c
World social economic planning 46

Bruno Zuckermann 23
*Zur Geschichte und Statistik des
   Volksschulwesens im In- und Auslande*
   102c